SEA TURTLES

Jeff Ripple

Voyageur Press

Edited by Todd R. Berger
Printed in Hong Kong

RINCA

96   97   98   99   00   5   4   3   2

Library of Congress Cataloging-in-Publication Data
Ripple, Jeff, 1963–
Sea turtles / by Jeff Ripple.
p.   cm. — (World life library)
Includes bibliographical references (p. 83) and index.
ISBN 0-89658-315-5
1. Sea turtles. I. Title. II. Series.
QL 666.C536R56   1996
597.92—dc20   95-22059
CIP

Distributed in Canada by Raincoast Books, 8680 Cambie Street, Vancouver, B.C. V6P 6M9

Published by Voyageur Press, Inc.
123 North Second Street, P.O. Box 338, Stillwater, MN 55082 U.S.A.
612-430-2210, fax 612-430-2211

Please write or call, or stop by, for our free catalog of natural history publications. Our toll-free number to place an order or to obtain a free catalog is 800-888-WOLF (800-888-9653).

Educators, fundraisers, premium and gift buyers, publicists, and marketing managers: Looking for creative products and new sales ideas? Voyageur Press books are available at special discounts when purchased in quantities, and special editions can be created to your specifications. For details contact our marketing department.

Photo page one: copyright © George H. H. Huey
Photo page four copyright © Doug Perrine/Innerspace Visions–Miami
Front cover photo: copyright © Doug Perrine/Innerspace Visions–Miami
Back cover photo copyright © Burt Jones/Maurine Shimlock–Secret Visions™

Dedicated to the memory of Dr. Archie Carr, Jr., a pioneer in sea turtle conservation and research, and to the many scientists, students, and volunteers who devote their lives to sea turtles.

Acknowledgments

I am grateful for the assistance provided by the following individuals and organizations during the research and writing of this book: David Godfrey and Dr. Jeanne Mortimer of the Sea Turtle Survival League/Caribbean Conservation Corporation, Dr. Blair Witherington of the Florida Department of Environmental Protection, Dr. Peter C. H. Pritchard of the Florida Audubon Society, Dr. Brian Bowen of the BEECS Genetic Analysis Core at the University of Florida, the Florida Department of Environmental Protection, the National Oceanic and Atmospheric Administration (NOAA), The Archie Carr Center for Sea Turtle Research at the University of Florida, The Nature Conservancy, the Center for Marine Conservation, the Sea Turtle Preservation Society, and the National Marine Fisheries Service. David Godfrey and members of the staff at the Sea Turtle Survival League/Caribbean Conservation Corporation, Blair Witherington, and Peter C. H. Pritchard reviewed the manuscript, and I am indebted to them for their suggestions and comments. Special thanks to my wife Renée for her enthusiastic help in the field and in the library, as well as for her editorial comments and constant support. I would also like to thank John Adkins, a really special kid who took the author's photograph near Cedar Key, Florida.

Table of Contents

An adult male loggerhead turtle swims through clear, shallow waters surrounding the Bahamas. (Photo © Doug Perrine/ Innerspace Visions–Miami)

Introduction: A Sea Turtle's Tale

It is July, and a female loggerhead turtle waits in the swells near shore as a full moon rises above the Atlantic. Daylight faded on the western horizon nearly an hour ago, and now the moonlight is gaining strength, shimmering along the tops of incoming waves as they spill over the sand, flooding the beach and tidal surge with a silky radiance. A few stars twinkle faintly overhead, nearly overpowered by the lunar glow.

The female mated in June with a male loggerhead in the shallow waters off Melbourne Beach, Florida. Most of the male turtles are gone now, having departed for their feeding grounds at the end of June, leaving the hundreds of females to lay their eggs in the warm sand of the beach. Only the females venture ashore, but not all at once. Rather, they straggle in a few at a time, each turtle somehow aware that she herself was hatched on this beach so many years ago.

This female nested once before this season, but now she senses the time is right for her to return to the beach and repeat her exhausting task. She rises to the surface of the sea and snatches a breath, and then submerges, barely needing to flap her long front flippers as the waves sweep her toward shore. Her belly bumps the sandy bottom, and the swell on which she rides washes over her and surges up the beach with a dull *whoosh*. With no water beneath her, her smooth swimming stroke changes to a labored, lizardlike crawl as she drags her immense bulk to the waterline, where she stops.

To an observer on shore she might appear as a low, dark shadow against the frothing surf, easily mistaken for a large rock. For ten minutes she watches and waits, suspicious of the unfamiliar element beneath her and the long stretch of beach in front of her. Finally, she begins to creep forward, slowly at first and then a little faster, with more purpose. Halfway up the beach she pauses again, blinks, and looks around. Two nights before she had come this far and abruptly turned around when curious human onlookers unwittingly caused her to change her mind and head back to sea. But tonight, the beach is deserted. She sighs heavily and pushes on toward the dune, the white sand glowing in the moonlight.

About twenty feet from the base of the dune, well above the high-tide line, she stops for a third time. Again she waits before she slowly begins to rock her body back and forth, throwing little heaps of sand to each side with her front flippers. She digs for more than fifteen minutes until firmly entrenched in a shallow pit, her head pointed toward the dune. Once in place, she begins to dig an egg chamber (shaped much like

A female green turtle returns to sea after laying her eggs on a beach in Malaysia. The track of a sea turtle is so distinctive that researchers can usually identify the species without actually seeing the turtle that made it. (Photo © Burt Jones/Maurine Shimlock—Secret Sea Visions™)

a physician's bag) with her back flippers, using them in alternating strokes like scoops to lift sand out and pile it behind her. Her shell rises and falls as she works. Thirty minutes elapse before the cavity is complete, and she then slowly deposits her leathery, ping-pong-ball–sized eggs, letting them slip into the hole two or three at a time, followed by a stream of mucus. Occasionally, she sighs and stops to rest. Tears well and drip down

the sides of her head as her body rids itself of excess salt through special glands near her eyes. After laying about 120 eggs, she is through.

Now she begins to cover the nest by pulling sand into the cavity with her back flippers. Once she has filled the hole, she pulls sand from around the body pit with long sweeps of her front flippers, concealing the location of the nest. After ten minutes of raking the sand, she raises her head and rotates her body to look up the length of the beach. Which way to the open sea? The surf sparkles under the moon's bright glow, and in that instant her direction becomes clear. The loggerhead crawls toward the surf, and within a few minutes she feels the water slide beneath her once again. She

Emerging from an egg roughly the size of a ping-pong ball, this tiny logger-head hatchling may grow into an adult measuring forty inches (102 cm) in length and weighing 350 pounds (159 kg). The egg and hatchling are from a hatchery at Cape Florida State Park, Key Biscayne, Florida. (Photo © Doug Perrine/Innerspace Visions–Miami)

is free to swim. Flapping her powerful front flippers like a bird, she flies through the shallows, the top of her shell silhouetted briefly against the moonlit waves, before disappearing beneath the surface. The ritual is complete.

Loggerheads are one of eight currently recognized species of sea turtle in the world, all of which are air-breathing reptiles superbly adapted to their marine environment. While sea turtles may resemble other turtles in many respects, there are important differences. Every sea turtle has paddle-shaped fore and hind flippers that enable it to "fly" birdlike through the water. The fore flippers are used mainly for stroking and power, while the hind flippers act as rudders for steering. A sea turtle's shell is more streamlined and flexible than most other turtles', which allows it to move through the water with greater speed and efficiency. Furthermore, the top of a sea turtle's skull is armored, which, along with the turtle's large size, helps compensate for the protection lost by its inability to pull its head into its shell like other turtles. Adult sea turtles have also lost the ability to right themselves if they get tipped over on land, and large sea turtles (such as the leatherback) find it nearly impossible to back up, whether underwater or on land. However, like freshwater turtles, female sea turtles must return to land to nest, usually on sandy sub-tropical and tropical beaches.

Turtles and Humans

Sea turtles have long fascinated humans and have figured prominently in the mythology of many cultures. Seri Indians, who still live on the shores of the Gulf of California and include turtle meat as an important part of their diet, believe that the world began on the back of a gigantic leathery (leatherback) turtle. In the Miskito Cays off the eastern coast of Nicaragua, the story of a Turtle Mother, a benevolent spirit who acts as an intermediary between the worlds of animals and humans, still lingers.

Unfortunately, the spiritual significance of sea turtles has not saved them from heavy exploitation for both subsistence and commerce. Millions of sea turtles once roamed the earth's oceans, but now only hundreds of thousands remain. Within the past five centuries, trade in sea turtle meat, eggs, shells, oil, and leather has driven almost every species to the brink of extinction. While many countries now strictly regulate this trade or ban it altogether, other factors contribute to a continued decline in sea turtle populations. Thousands of sea turtles drown each year in shrimp nets, gill nets, and on the hooks of long lines. Others get tangled in monofilament, ground up in dredges, or die after ingesting plastic, mistaking it for jellyfish, a common food for some species. Development of oceanfront property has destroyed nesting beaches worldwide, leaving turtles with fewer places to lay their eggs.

As a result of the marked reduction in their numbers, the loggerhead, leatherback, green, Kemp's ridley, and hawksbill—five species of sea turtles found in the waters of the United States—are listed under the U.S.

A juvenile loggerhead turtle dives after snatching a breath at the ocean surface.
(Photo © Doug Perrine/Innerspace Visions—Miami)

A female leatherback turtle during a rare daylight nesting occurrence on a French Guiana beach. Sea turtles generally nest under cover of darkness for protection against predators and to escape the heat of the sun. (Photo © Peter C. H. Pritchard)

Endangered Species Act (ESA) of 1973 as either threatened or endangered. The U.S. Department of the Interior and the U.S. Department of Commerce are implementing recovery plans for these species, but sea turtles do not recognize national borders, and their conservation is increasingly becoming an international responsibility. Fortunately, concern for the plight of sea turtles is strong and growing stronger, with an international cadre of dedicated volunteers, conservationists, government agencies, and public and private organizations working to protect sea turtles on their nesting beaches and at sea. Researchers do more research each year to explore the natal homing instinct of nesting females, sea turtle migrations, navigation, body temperature regulation, diving and anoxic capabilities, and other fascinating mysteries surrounding these animals. Thousands of people volunteer to help with beach patrols and nest programs each year, while thousands more attend "turtle walks" in the hopes of seeing sea turtles come ashore to nest. Perhaps a focused preservation effort by the international community can restore sea turtles to numbers approaching their former abundance. There is still time—but precious little of it—to ensure that the ancient spectacle of a female loggerhead digging her nest on a moonlit, sandy beach will be a memorable event for future generations of turtles and humans. I hope this book will contribute to that effort.

A green sea turtle swims near Grand Cayman Island. (Photo © Doug Perrine/Innerspace Visions–Miami)

Ancient Nomads in a Modern Sea

Turtles have lived on earth for more than two hundred million years. In that time, they have changed little. Their origins remain a mystery, although there is some evidence linking them to an extinct line of lizardlike reptiles that had accumulated bony material in the skin of the back. The first fossil records of sea turtles, from about 150 million years ago, show many characteristics of modern turtles, including fully developed shells. This early fossil evidence indicates that they probably evolved from marsh-dwelling species.

By the late Cretaceous Period (approximately 65 to 70 million years ago), sea turtles had evolved into four distinct families (Toxochelidae, Protostegidae, Cheloniidae, and Dermochelyidae) and were distributed throughout the world's oceans. Of these four families, only the Cheloniidae (the hard-shelled sea turtles) and Dermochelyidae (the leatherback sea turtle) remain. Modern sea turtles, though less specialized and diverse than their ancestors, are the only living group of reptiles that spend their lives in a marine environment, with the exception of a few species of sea snakes.

General Characteristics

Although each species of sea turtle is distinctive in appearance and behavior, all sea turtles have certain characteristics in common. The shell consists of an upper part (the carapace) and a lower part (the plastron), which are joined together by cartilage to protect the vulnerable internal organs. In most species, keratinous scutes (scales) cover the carapace. Biologists note the number and arrangement of the scutes to identify species. Sea turtles do not have teeth, but their jaws have become modified into "beaks" to crush, tear, or bite, depending on their diet. Like all turtles, they lack external ears, and their eardrums are covered by skin. They hear best at lower frequencies, and their sense of smell is excellent. Though their vision underwater is good, above water they are nearsighted.

Sea turtles spend most of their time submerged but periodically rise to the surface to breathe. A single explosive exhalation and quick inhalation are all that is required to replenish their oxygen supply. Their lungs have adapted to permit a rapid exchange of oxygen and to prevent gasses from being trapped during deep dives. During routine activity, turtles dive for about four to five minutes and surface to breathe for one to three seconds. Turtles can rest or sleep underwater for several hours at a time, but their ability to hold their breath is considerably shortened by heightened activity or stress. This is why sea turtles drown in shrimp nets and other fishing gear within a relatively short time. Many adult sea turtles sleep near rocks or under ledges. Hatchlings and juveniles sleep on the surface with their front flippers swept back over the carapace.

Temperature and Sea Turtles

Like other reptiles, most sea turtles are susceptible to extremes in temperature because they cannot maintain a constant internal temperature the way mammals and other warm-blooded creatures do. When winter water temperatures dip below 59°F (15°C), most sea turtles become lethargic and will either seek warmer water or burrow into the mud to hibernate. Scientists were unaware that some sea turtles hibernate until the 1970s, when they discovered, buried in the mud of deep channels, torpid Pacific green turtles near Baja California and Atlantic loggerheads off Cape Canaveral on Florida's east coast. Water temperatures that drop below 41°F (5°C) for more than twelve hours can be lethal to sea turtles, as documented by the deaths of several cold-stunned turtles stranded in the Mosquito Lagoon-Indian River estuary on Florida's east coast. Winter strandings of turtles have also been reported from Texas, western Europe, New England, and New York's Long Island Sound.

Overheating can be just as dangerous for sea turtles as extreme cold. Sunlight (even through cloud cover) can cause a rapid rise (as much as 18°F or 10°C) in the body temperature of a large turtle, especially during the heavy physical exertion involved with nesting. This—as well as the obvious danger of predation—is why most sea turtle nesting occurs at night. A large sea turtle such as a green or a loggerhead that nests during the day runs the risk of not being able to complete nesting due to heat stress. After nesting, a large turtle unable to get back to the ocean within a short period of time will almost always die of heat stroke. However, small sea turtles, such as the Kemp's and olive ridleys, regularly nest during the day. Why is this? Because ridleys are such small sea turtles, they cool more quickly than do large species, especially under windy conditions. Daytime nestings of the ridleys are always associated with strong breezes that prevent the turtles from overheating.

Feeding Habits During the Stages of Life

Sea turtles may use different feeding areas at each stage of growth. For example, the hatchlings of virtually all species are believed to head out toward the open ocean from their natal beach. At sea, they take up residence in rafts of sargassum weeds or other flotsam caught in convergence zones of surface currents. Here they typically dine on macroplankton, small snails and crustaceans, and other invertebrates. After several

*This coral crest on a reef off the coast of Indonesia provides a green turtle with an ideal place to rest.
(Photo © Burt Jones/Maurine Shimlock—Secret Sea Visions™)*

A sharksucker (Echeneis naucrates) hitches a ride on a male loggerhead turtle as it cruises the Atlantic near the Bahamas. (Photo © Doug Perrine/ Innerspace Visions—Miami)

A loggerhead turtle swims through clear water off the Bahamas. (Photo © Doug Perrine/Innerspace Visions—Miami)

years of riding the currents as juveniles, they venture into nearshore areas and estuaries to continue their development to adulthood. Once they reach adulthood, they move into the traditional feeding areas they will use for the rest of their lives. No one knows for sure what prompts their movement from juvenile feeding grounds to those of the adults.

Growth and Age

Growth rates among sea turtles vary. In general, they mature slowly and are believed to have relatively long life spans, perhaps as long as seventy-five to one hundred years.

During the first few years of life, a juvenile sea turtle grows quickly. For example, a young green turtle, no larger than a half dollar (50 mm) at birth, may each month add between five and fourteen ounces (130–400 g) to its hatching weight and approximately .3 to .4 inch (8–10 mm) to its carapace length. By the time a juvenile green turtle is three and a half years old, it may weigh about twenty-two pounds (10 kg) and measure fourteen inches (35 cm) in carapace length.

As a sea turtle matures, its growth rate slows. Adult green turtles, hawksbills, and loggerheads increase less than a half-inch (13 mm) in length each year. In addition, there is great variation in the size of individuals at the time they breed and nest for the first time. In other words, the largest turtles on the nesting beach are not necessarily the oldest.

Sea turtles reach sexual maturity at ages ranging from about seven years in captive turtles to nearly fifty in wild turtles, depending on the species and the quality of the habitat in which the turtles feed. Captive sea turtles that have been fed special high-protein diets grow faster and mature much more quickly than wild turtles, whose diet is typically low in nutrients.

The length of the carapace is one indicator biologists use to tell where a turtle is in its life cycle. A sea turtle's length is recorded by using a tape measure or calipers to measure from the front edge of the carapace to the rear edge—not from the tip of the beak to the tip of the tail.

Navigation and Migration

Most sea turtles regularly undertake long migrations between their feeding grounds and nesting beaches. No one is sure how they find their way. Several theories have been offered, such as that turtles navigate by the stars, sun, or polarized light; they determine latitude by sensing the speed of the earth's rotation or degree of inclination angle; or they follow the gradient of a particular taste or smell emanating from rivers and coastlines. According to Dr. Ken Lohmann of the University of North Carolina, sea turtles possess a magnetic inclination compass that enables them to distinguish poleward direction and latitude. This might have something to do with small amounts of magnetite found in the brain. Turtles may use a variety of cues or mechanisms, depending on whether they are traveling through the open ocean, navigating a coastline, or homing in on a particular stretch of beach. Regardless of the number and diversity of theories, most of what we know is still conjecture, and the great migrations of sea turtles and other far-ranging creatures remain among the natural world's most compelling mysteries.

Immature green sea turtles crowd together in a tank at the Cayman Turtle Farm in the Cayman Islands. This turtle farm is one of the few facilities in the world where green turtles are raised and legally harvested for their meat and calipee. (Photo © Doug Perrine/Innerspace Visions–Miami)

Natural Predation

The first few moments out of the nest are possibly the most dangerous in a turtle's life. Predators abound, and many hatchlings don't even make it to the surge line. Ants, ghost crabs, foxes, coyotes, vultures, coatis, raccoons, and feral pigs and dogs are just a few of the creatures that eat eggs and hatchlings. Bacteria in the nests destroy many eggs before they hatch. Hatchlings that survive the beach must face a phalanx of finned predators waiting for them in the sea. Darkness provides some protection, but not much. Hatchlings that emerge during daylight rarely get very far, because birds such as terns, gulls, and frigatebirds make short work of them. It is no wonder that the odds of a hatchling surviving to reproduce as an adult are less than one in a thousand.

Fortunately, the large size and hard carapace of adult sea turtles make them less suitable prey for most animals. Sharks and orcas (killer whales) probably account for a few adult turtle deaths; jaguars have occasionally killed nesting females on tropical South American beaches.

Human-Caused Mortality

Human beings are by far the most dangerous enemy of sea turtles. We value the eggs of all sea turtle species directly as food or as ingredients in baked goods, and in some Latin American and Asian countries, the eggs are believed to be aphrodisiacs. Green turtle meat and soup are considered gourmet cuisine in many parts of the world. Olive ridleys are killed for the skin of the neck, shoulders, and flippers, which, when tanned, is exported to Europe and Asia to be converted into fine leather purses, shoes, and boots. The shells of hawksbills—the source of natural tortoiseshell or *carey*—are fashioned into ornately carved rings and hair clips, earrings, combs, and other decorative items. Complete shells are lacquered for use as wall hangings, and entire juvenile turtles are stuffed and sold to tourists, sometimes with tropical scenes painted on their backs. Leatherbacks were once rendered for their oil for use in lamps and may still be used in some cosmetics.

Historically, taking eggs or killing turtles, for the most part, was at a subsistence level by indigenous cultures and had little impact on overall turtle populations. Within the last few hundred years, however, a commercial demand for sea turtle products developed and has since pushed most species down a path toward extinction. In the Caribbean alone, where, at one time, green turtles probably were more numerous than they were anywhere else on earth, fishermen supplying the European markets with green turtles for meat and soup eliminated eight of the original ten distinct breeding populations in less than three hundred years. Today, the once glorious mass nesting of Kemp's ridley turtles has shrunk to a mere fraction of its former size because of the demand for eggs and the loss of adults in shrimp nets. Hawksbills are probably more common as wall hangings than as living creatures in the wild. Many indigenous cultures, for which the gathering of eggs or the killing of a turtle was once governed by taboo or tradition, have been forced to convert to cash-based economies. Turtles are now regarded less as gifts from the ocean than as commodities for the taking.

Our impact on sea turtles is both direct (intentional take) and indirect (accidental take). Direct exploitation usually involves the harvesting of eggs for food or for sale at market. Most countries forbid the taking of eggs, but enforcement is lax, poaching is rampant, and the eggs are frequently offered for sale in local markets without consequence. Turtle populations in many areas of the world are declining rapidly as a result. Populations of olive ridleys continue to dwindle because of egg poaching and the illegal trade of their skins and meat. Japan, which imported 1.4 million pounds of hawksbill scutes (this translates to 600,000 animals) between 1970 and 1986, agreed to end this practice in 1992, but U.S. Customs and U.S. Fish and Wildlife Service personnel still regularly confiscate whole turtles and products made from hawksbill shell, much of it

Most national governments prohibit the taking of turtle eggs from nests. Unfortunately, enforcement is often difficult, and the poaching of eggs and sea turtles is a global problem. Here, a poacher steals eggs from a green turtle nest on a beach in Malaysia. (Photo © Burt Jones/Maurine Shimlock–Secret Sea Visions™)

Olive ridley eggs bagged and ready to go to market at Ostional, Costa Rica. In rare instances, turtle eggs are gathered and sold at markets legally. Controlled harvests of eggs, such as the collecting of olive ridley eggs at Ostional, benefit the local community and encourage residents to protect nests from poachers and the hatchlings from predators. Most turtle colonies, however, cannot afford to lose even a few nests, and the project at Ostional is considered a unique situation. (Photo © Peter C. H. Pritchard) from the Caribbean. Fortunately, most green turtle meat and calipee now come from a green turtle farm in the Grand Cayman Islands, which exports its products for European consumption.

Our indirect impact is more insidious, but equally widespread and detrimental to the survival of all sea turtles. Some of the most significant causes of indirect mortality are highlighted below.

Commercial Fishing. Worldwide, trawling probably accounts for the incidental death of more juvenile and adult sea turtles than any other source. According to a May 1990 National Academy of Sciences (NAS) study, as many as fifty-five thousand sea turtles (five thousand of which are Kemp's ridleys) are killed each year in shrimp nets in the southeastern United States alone. In this study, scientists estimated that this senseless carnage could be reduced by as much as 97 percent if the nets were fitted with Turtle Excluder Devices (TEDs), tow times for the nets were reduced to under fifty minutes, and time and area closures were authorized during periods of nesting or other aggregations. A TED is any of a variety of grids that can be placed in the throat of a shrimp net to allow debris, turtles, and other large marine animals to escape the nets without significantly reducing the take of shrimp. Sea turtles rarely die if they are brought to the surface within fifty minutes of their capture, and during certain times of the year they are not present in areas regularly trawled by shrimp boats.

In December 1994, regulations requiring the use of TEDs in all waters of the southeastern United States were implemented. As of this writing (May 1995), new figures for the number of sea turtle deaths attributed to shrimp nets are not yet available, but researchers expect far fewer deaths now that the TED regulations are in effect.

According to the 1990 NAS study, other fisheries (e.g., those that use drift nets, long lines, sturgeon nets, and other such gear) account for roughly five thousand loggerhead and five hundred Kemp's ridley deaths each year in the United States. As much as 150,000 tons (135,000 metric tons) of gear—including plastic nets, lines, and buoys with anchoring lines—is lost or discarded annually. Many turtles are found trapped in abandoned gill nets, become entangled in discarded monofilament, or are caught on long lines set for sharks or swordfish.

Ingestion of Nondegradable Debris and Plastics. An estimated one to two million birds and more than one hundred thousand marine mammals and sea turtles die from eating or becoming entangled in nondegradable debris each year, including packing bands, balloons, pellets, bottles, vinyl films, tarballs, and Styrofoam. Plastic bags and balloons resemble jellyfish and other prey, and when turtles ingest these, they can cause stomach and intestinal blockage, killing the turtles by starvation or by infection.

Beach Armoring. There are several types of beach armoring, including sea walls, rock revetments, riprap, sandbag installations, groins, and jetties. Beach armoring can result in a permanent loss of dry nesting beach through accelerated erosion and prevention of natural beach and sand accretion. They can deter or altogether prevent female turtles from coming ashore to nest. As the structures fail or break apart, they spread debris on the beach, impeding access to suitable nesting sites. The result is a higher incidence of false crawls and the trapping of females and hatchlings, who perish while trying to get to the sea.

After a run off Port Canaveral, Florida, to test a Turtle Excluder Device (TED), National Marine Fisheries Service personnel compare catches from a shrimp net equipped with a TED (left) and a net trawled without a TED (right). Note the three sea turtles and large number of fish taken from the net trawled without the TED. This bycatch is considered waste and is thrown overboard, usually dead. The net with the TED yielded significantly less bycatch. (Photo © Ian K. Workman)

Beach Renourishment. Beach renourishment is pumping, trucking, or otherwise depositing sand on a beach to replace what has eroded away. Beach renourishment can severely compact the sand, and the sand that is imported is sometimes different from native beach sediments, thereby potentially affecting nest-site selection, digging behavior, incubation temperature, gas-exchange characteristics in incubating nests, and the moisture content of nests. All of these factors can affect sex ratio and hatching success.

Artificial Lighting. Artificial beachfront lights from buildings, streetlights, dune crossovers or boardwalks, vehicles, campfires, flashlights, and other sources disorient hatchlings. Studies of female loggerhead and green turtles indicate that females will generally avoid beach areas with bright lights. Striking a match on a dark night in the vicinity of an emerging green turtle can be enough to send her back to the sea.

Beach Raking. Mechanical raking with heavy machinery such as tractors or buggies can crush nests or hatchlings waiting to emerge, and hand rakes can disturb sealed nests. Sometimes, the only reason for extensive nest relocation programs is because of mechanical raking.

Increased Human Presence on Nesting Beaches. During the nesting season, heavy nighttime visitation to beaches can cause turtles to shift to other nesting beaches, delay egg-laying, and select poor nesting sites. There is a higher incidence of false crawls on nights where there is heavy human use of the beach. Campfires and shining flashlights on the beach will deter females from nesting and disorient hatchlings.

Beach Driving. People are still allowed to drive vehicles on some beaches in the United States along the Gulf of Mexico and Atlantic Ocean year-round, including during the turtle nesting season. Headlights can disrupt the nesting process and disorient hatchlings. Hatchlings are accidentally run over as they race toward the sea. Hatchlings trapped in tire tracks in the sand expend precious energy reserves and increase their exposure on the beach. In some areas, beach driving is the only reason conservationists must relocate turtle nests.

Exotic Dune and Beach Vegetation. Exotic (nonnative) vegetation on nesting beaches has invaded or been planted in many coastal areas and frequently displaces native species, such as sea oats, beach morning glory, railroad vine, sea grape, dune panic grass, and pennywort. Exotics can destabilize dunes—thereby increasing erosion—or form impenetrable root mats, which can trap emerging hatchlings or prevent adults from properly excavating nest cavities. One particularly pesky exotic is the Australian pine (*Casuarina equisetifolia*), a species that has invaded many coastal strand areas of central and south Florida. The trees form dense stands that eliminate native dune plants and shade extensive areas of beach. They force turtles to use middle and lower beach areas more frequently, which increases the chances of tidal flooding of the nests. Shading lowers the sand temperature, affecting incubation times and the natural hatchling sex ratio. Fallen Australian pines prevent females from nesting and can trap females and hatchlings trying to reach the sea.

Mating, Nesting, Incubation, and Emergence

Most of what we know about sea turtles revolves around their behavior during nesting and their first few minutes of life as hatchlings racing from the nest to the sea. Researchers have traditionally focused their attention on these aspects of behavior because, with few exceptions, these are the only times when the animals are on shore, where they are accessible and can be easily observed. Sea turtles are generally solitary creatures that remain submerged for much of the time they are at sea, which makes them extremely difficult to study. They rarely interact with one another outside of courtship and mating and, for ridleys, the time of the *arribada*, when they come ashore en masse. Even when large numbers of turtles gather on feeding grounds or during migration, there is little behavioral exchange among individuals.

Courtship and mating for most sea turtles is believed to occur during a limited "receptive" period prior to the female's first emergence from the sea to nest. Only females come ashore to nest; males almost never return to land once they leave the sand of their natal beach.

Courtship and Mating. Male sea turtles are similar to females in size and color. However, a mature male, in most species, can be distinguished from a female by his long tail (a male's tail extends beyond the posterior edge of the carapace), longer recurved claws on the front and rear flippers, and slightly concave plastron. These external features are important in helping the male keep his grip on a female during mating. When a female has accepted a male, he grasps her by hooking his flipper claws around the forward edge of her carapace and curling his prehensile, spur-tipped tail beneath her plastron. His recurved flipper claws often leave gouges in the female's shell and deep lacerations in the skin of her shoulders. Mating is a slow process that can take place at the surface, on the bottom, or in the water column. The pair remains locked together for up to two hours, and any swimming or diving is undertaken entirely by the female since the male is preoccupied with holding on and maintaining his balance.

Courtship and mating among sea turtles is a tempestuous affair, with several males pursuing a female, although only one will successfully mate with her. The others stay in the vicinity of the mating pair, sometimes circling and biting the tail and flippers of the successful male, often causing extensive injuries. In the frenzy to mate, males may fight aggressively with each other, pursue large moving objects (including human divers), and attempt to dislodge mating males. Native fishermen take advantage of the male turtle's raging passions by setting out crude wooden decoys of the females, which the males readily accept. The fishermen then haul the decoys back to the boat, with the male turtles still attached.

A female turtle may not always be receptive to a male's advances. If she is not ready to mate, she will fold her hind flippers together or position herself vertically in the water column with her plastron facing the male, making it nearly impossible for him to mount her. In some regions, unreceptive females retreat to a reserve, a "no touching permitted" zone to which females withdraw when they do not want to be harassed by males. There they rest on the bottom sand. Males ignore all females in this area.

The receptive period varies among species, but studies with captive green turtles show that females are receptive to males for about thirty days prior to laying their first nest. Receptive females may produce pheromones (chemical attractants) to entice males during this period. Females store sperm throughout a nesting season, but there is no evidence that it can be retained to the next nesting season.

Sea walls and other types of beach armoring accelerate the loss of dry nesting beach and leave little suitable habitat for sea turtles to nest. As a result, female turtles are sometimes forced to go elsewhere to lay their eggs. (Photo © Marilyn Kazmers/ SharkSong)

A hawksbill turtle swims over soft coral in the Bahamas. (Photo © Doug Perrine/Innerspace Visions–Miami)

Green turtles mating, Malaysia. A male grasps the female by hooking the claws on his foreflippers around the anterior edge of her carapace and curling his prehensile, spur-tipped tail beneath her plastron. The turtles may remain locked in this embrace for up to two hours. (Photo © Burt Jones/ Maurine Shimlock–Secret Sea Visions™)

Beach Selection Theories. Why do sea turtles nest on some beaches, but not on others? That is a question for which there is no clear answer. Some scientists suggest that current nesting choices and rookery locations may reflect historic patterns that have existed for hundreds or thousands of years. Some suitable beaches may go untouched because the sea turtle population that once used them has disappeared, due either to overexploitation or possibly other unseen environmental factors. One thing is certain: Most females return faithfully to the same beach each time they are ready to nest. Not only do they appear on the same beach, they typically emerge within a few hundred yards of where they last nested. Dr. Archie Carr, Jr., a pioneer in sea turtle research, proposed the theory of natal homing to further explain this nest-site fidelity observed in adult females. His theory is that a female hatchling imprints on the unique qualities of a beach while still in the nest or during her first trip to the sea. Cues that can help her identify the beach include smell, low-frequency sound such as surf noise, magnetic fields, and the characteristics of seasonal offshore currents.

An alternative "social-facilitation" hypothesis by Dr. J. R. Hendrickson to explain nest-site fidelity by adult females suggested that first-time nesters learn the location of nesting beaches not by recognizing cues they learned as hatchlings, but by following experienced adults from feeding grounds to the rookery. However, tag returns and recent evidence from mitochondrial DNA analysis, presented by Dr. Brian Bowen and his colleagues, seem to support Carr's theory that most female sea turtles nest on their natal beaches. For reasons that are still unknown, a few females do choose to nest in new locations, thereby pioneering new rookeries for future generations. This is important for the long-term survival of the turtles, since an absolute adherence to traditional nesting rookeries would have long ago doomed sea turtles to extinction.

Over the years, tagging has been an essential research tool in proving or disproving various hypotheses about the migrations between sea turtle feeding grounds and nesting beaches. However, tagging methods used in the past to identify baby turtles were less than perfect for tracking hatchlings to adulthood. For example, a small plastic or metal tag applied to a flipper or the carapace drops off quickly as a hatchling grows. A notch cut in its carapace may resemble notches from shark attacks or other accidental injuries to the carapace that occur naturally over the course of the turtle's life.

A new technique, however, has been developed that may finally enable scientists to track turtles from birth to adulthood. This method is called the "living tag" and involves transplanting a small piece of plastron tissue to the carapace and simultaneously implanting a piece of carapace to the plastron. Since the carapace of adults is typically much darker than the plastron, a "tagged" turtle will always display a distinctive light patch on the carapace and a dark patch on the plastron that does not match its naturally occurring color pattern.

Sea turtles, especially large species such as the leatherback and loggerhead, seem to prefer beaches with open-water access. The beach must be elevated to prevent flooding by tides, rain, or groundwater, and the sand must be loose enough to allow for gas diffusion, yet be moist enough to prevent collapse during digging. Other factors that may determine where a turtle nests are beach slope, sand texture, the presence of offshore reefs, dune vegetation, artificial lighting, and human activity on the beach. The location of a nest is critical to the development and survival of eggs and hatchlings. If a nest is too close to the water, it could be flooded by the tide, and the eggs will fail to develop. If it is too far up on the beach, roots from vegetation can invade the nest, predators are more likely to ravage the nest, and hatchlings will have a longer journey to the surf.

Nesting Behavior. Most females nest at least twice during a given mating season, although individuals of some species may nest only once and others as many as ten or eleven times. Sea turtles are generally heavy, slow, and awkward on land, and nesting is exhausting work. Ridleys and hawksbills are more mobile than other sea turtles because of their smaller size, and they move around the beach like little tanks, sometimes raising themselves on their flippers to scramble about on the sand. Loggerheads, hawksbills, and both species of ridleys move on land with a lizardlike gait in which the diagonal limbs move simultaneously. Leatherbacks and green turtles, however, drag themselves forward by moving the opposite limbs together. By using the tracks in the sand made as a result of each turtle's distinctive gait, researchers can identify which species nested without actually seeing the turtle.

Tracking studies with loggerheads show that when they are ready to nest, they move into the surf off the nesting beach in the late afternoon and early evening to wait until it is dark. A turtle may stop several times to shove her snout into the sand as she emerges from the water and proceeds up the beach. Her reasons for doing this are unclear, although it has been suggested that she might be following a temperature gradient from the cool, wet sand near the water to the warmer, dry beach zone to select a suitable nest site, or that she could be appraising the smell, texture, or water content of the sand.

If a female crawls onto the beach, but does not nest, she will return to the water and swim parallel to the beach in the surf zone until deciding to attempt another emergence. If she nests successfully, she swims away from the beach to a shoal area. The time spent on the beach varies among species and ranges from less than an hour to more than two hours.

A black turtle hatchling struggles to free itself from a ghost crab, one of its many predators. Ghost crabs disable hatchlings by snipping the tendons in the front flippers. A single ghost crab may disable several hatchlings in this manner and then later drag them into its burrow to eat them. (Photo © George H. H. Huey)

Once a nest site has been chosen, the turtle clears the area by sweeping it with her front flippers, although all four flippers are sometimes used. She then excavates a body pit by digging with her flippers and rotating her body. This removes unstable dry sand that would collapse during the digging and allows the female to place the egg cavity farther from the surface. After the body pit is complete, the female digs an egg cavity using her cupped rear flippers as shovels. All sea turtles alternate their hind limbs as they dig. After one rear flipper removes a scoop of sand, the other shoots forward to spread sand to the side and front. The egg cavity is shaped much like a physician's bag and is usually tilted slightly. Its final depth is determined by the combined depth of the body pit and the length of the female's rear flippers.

A number of factors can affect whether or not a turtle will complete nest construction and begin laying eggs. Many turtles emerging from the water, ascending the beach, or digging a nest cavity may turn back if they are bothered by lights or by unusual activity on the beach. Some turtles will abandon a nest site if they encounter a root, rock, or other obstacle, or if the sand does not have the correct consistency or moisture content. Other turtles may nest regardless of what is going on around them. If a turtle fails to nest and returns to the sea from the beach without laying her eggs, it is referred to as a "false crawl." The percentage of false crawls varies among species, among populations within a species, and even among individuals within specific populations.

It is a popular belief that when a sea turtle begins to lay her eggs, she goes into a trance in which she is oblivious to what happens around her. This is not entirely true. A sea turtle is least likely to abandon nesting when she is laying her eggs, but some turtles will abandon the process if they are harassed or feel they are in serious danger. For this reason, it is important that great care is taken when observing all phases of sea turtle nesting. Once a female has left her nest, complete or not, she never returns to attend it.

When the turtle has completed the egg chamber, she begins to lay eggs. Two or three eggs are deposited at a time, with mucus being secreted between batches of eggs. The average size of a clutch ranges from 80 to 120 eggs, depending on the species. Because the eggs are leathery and flexible, they do not break as they fall into the chamber. The turtle often rests between batches of eggs. Nesting sea turtles appear to shed tears, but these salty secretions are produced continuously and just happen to be visible during nesting.

The large number of eggs sea turtles produce has earned them the moniker "egg-laying machines." In the wild, most adult female sea turtles will lay several hundred eggs during a nesting season. Clutch size for each species is a compromise that reflects many factors such as the need to compensate for high predation, space limitations inside the turtle's shell, and the size of the nest cavity.

Depending on the species of turtle, as much as two-thirds of the time involved in nesting takes place after the eggs have been laid. The female spends this time covering and disguising the nest. She uses her rear flippers to rake and pack sand into the open nest cavity. After compressing the sand over the cavity with her body, the female conceals the nest site with long swipes of her front flippers. She then heads back down the beach past the breakers to the safety of the sea.

A metal tag on the flipper of a loggerhead turtle, Azores Islands. Tagging is one method scientists use to track sea turtles to learn about their migrations from nesting beaches to feeding grounds. (Photo © Doug Perrine/Innerspace Visions—Miami)

Nest temperature is critical in determining the incubation period and the sex of growing sea turtle embryos. Incubation generally takes about eight weeks, but since the temperature of the sand governs the speed at which the embryos develop, the hatching period can range remarkably. Essentially, the hotter the sand surrounding the nest, the faster the embryos develop. Shallow nests laid in unshaded, open beach locations may be heated by temperatures above 95°F (35°C). These nests may take only forty-two to forty-five days to hatch. However, deep nests and those located in shady areas will take much longer, possibly up to sixty-five days. As a result, nests laid on the same night, but in different places on the beach, may not hatch at the same time.

Perhaps the most fascinating effect of nest temperature on sea turtle eggs is how it impacts the sex of the embryos. Green turtles, and possibly all sea turtles, have no heteromorphic sex chromosomes, which in most animals carry the genetic material that determines whether an embryo will become a male or a female. Temperature-dependent sex determination (TSD) has been observed in loggerhead, green, leatherback, and olive ridley turtles. The molecular mechanisms responsible for this phenomenon are unknown, but the results are fairly uniform. The critical time for sex determination occurs during the middle third of incubation. According to studies on green turtles by S. J. Morreale, temperatures below 82.4°F (28°C) produce 90 to 100 percent males, temperatures between 83.3°F (28.5°C) and 86.4°F (30.2°C) produce increased numbers of females, and temperatures of 86.9°F (30.5°C) or higher produce 94 to 100 percent females. In a 1985 article in *Copeia*, Edward A. Standora and James R. Spotila suggest that during this period, factors such as osmotic stress, as well as oxygen and carbon dioxide levels, could influence the sex of the embryos to a lesser degree.

Nest location influences sex determination and incubation time because it affects the temperature within the nest. A 1.8°F (1°C) decrease in temperature from shading or excessive rain may add five days to the incubation period and, if it occurs during the critical middle third of incubation, could impact the ratio of males to females within the nest. Some scientists believe that the location of eggs within the nest can also influence the sex of developing embryos because of metabolic heating. For example, eggs in the center of the clutch—where it is warmer—will turn out more females, while eggs on the outside perimeter of the clutch will produce predominately males.

An immature loggerhead turtle with a "living tag," as well as two conventional metal tags. The living tag—a piece of light-colored plastron tissue implanted on the carapace—will allow scientists to track this turtle throughout its life. (Photo © Doug Perrine/Innerspace Visions–Miami)

The ratio of male to female hatchlings may also vary with the seasons. In a study of green turtles at Tortuguero, Costa Rica, nests laid during the monsoon season (December and January) yielded primarily males and those laid between April and November turned out mainly females. Due in part to these seasonal variations, there may be a propensity for some beaches to regularly produce more of one sex than the other. For example, because most males hatch from clutches laid between December and January, and more females hatch from clutches laid between April and November, the primary sex ratio of the Tortuguero beach is biased towards females, with an overall production of approximately 74 percent females for the entire year.

Considering the importance of temperature on sex determination and incubation time, how might the efforts of sea turtle hatchery programs affect the overall success of turtle rookeries? It has been common practice at many nesting locations to transplant nests from natural sites on the beach to Styrofoam boxes in protected hatcheries when poaching, predators, or high tides might otherwise destroy the eggs. Incubation temperatures in Styrofoam boxes, however, are usually cooler than in natural nests, and it now seems clear that many efforts to protect nests and increase the hatchling production during the last twenty-five years may have yielded far too many male turtles. Over time, rookeries could become extinct because not enough

A loggerhead turtle drops its eggs into the nest cavity. The eggs are leathery and flexible, so they don't break when they fall. (Photo © Marilyn Kazmers/SharkSong)

A green turtle digs its nest on a beach in Indonesia. (Photo © Burt Jones/Maurine Shimlock—Secret Sea Visions™)

Black turtle hatchlings enter the surf on a beach in Michoacan, Mexico. Hatchlings are strongly attracted to light, a trait that enables them to find the ocean—generally the brightest and most open horizon (on undeveloped beaches)—even on the darkest night. (Photo © George H. H. Huey)

females are produced in the hatcheries to return to the beaches to nest.

Unlike baby alligators, which are liberated from their nest by their mother and then carried gently to the water in her mouth, sea turtle hatchlings are on their own from the moment their mother finishes covering the nest. Digging out of the nest is a group effort that can take several days. It is rare that only one or two hatchlings escape from the sand by themselves. In a typical nest, when the first hatchling has ripped open its leathery eggshell with its egg tooth (a sharp temporary extension of the upper jaw that drops off soon after birth), its movement in the nest stimulates others to begin hatching. Within twelve hours after the first turtle wriggles free from its shell, most of the babies that have developed successfully are out of their shells as well. At this time, each hatchling still has a yolk sack attached to the outside of its body. This sack must be completely absorbed into the body and the umbilical opening closed before the turtle reaches the surface. Otherwise, the hatchling will not survive. The yolk remaining in the hatchling will continue to nourish it during its first few days of life outside the nest.

The rise to the surface of the nest is a blindly cooperative effort among the siblings that involves sporadic bursts of thrashing, usually triggered by one turtle and quickly spreading through the clutch. The thrashing turtles dislodge sand from the walls and ceiling of the nest chamber, building up the floor and gradually raising the hatchlings to within a few inches of the surface. The rapid heating of the sand during the day brings a halt to all thrashing, so it may take two or three nights for the mass of sea turtles to move slowly but steadily to the surface. When the hatchlings get close to the top of the cavity, the sand sinks in a circular area above the nest. Now the young turtles are in position to emerge from the cavity.

Hatchlings usually emerge from their nest at night or during a rainstorm in response to cooling surface temperatures. If it is too hot outside the nest, the hatchlings nearest the surface stop moving, and this lack of activity has a quieting effect on the baby turtles below them. However, once they decide to burst out, they literally erupt from the nest cavity. Once on the beach, the little turtles scramble around the top opening of the nest, orient themselves, and then dash toward the sea.

A hatchling sea turtle is about the size of a half dollar. How do the hatchlings know where to go when, from their Lilliputian perspective of less than two inches (5 cm) above the surface, all they see are rolling hills and valleys of sand? Footprints, tire tracks, the moats of sand castles, beach debris—all are formidable obstacles that must be overcome. Hatchlings are strongly attracted to light and push relentlessly toward the brightest part of the horizon, even on a moonless night. They also instinctively orient themselves away from

tall silhouettes, such as dunes or dark buildings. On an undeveloped turtle beach, this poses no problem, since the lightest and most open horizon is typically over the ocean. Unfortunately, on beaches with ocean-front development, artificial lighting striking the beach can confuse hatchlings, sometimes leading them to an early death amidst dune vegetation or on busy streets.

Hatchlings scrambling down the beach constantly bump each other, the activity of one stimulating others in the group to move as quickly as possible across the dangerous sand. Once the hatchlings reach the water, they must negotiate the surf. The tiny turtles instinctively know how to swim. The first taste of ocean they encounter is the shallow sheet flow of a spent wave, which lifts each turtle slightly, and instantly the crawling motion is replaced by the typical flapping swim strokes. As the next breaking wave nears the beach, each turtle dives to the bottom and rides the undertow out to the calm water beyond the breaker. This diving response prevents the hatchlings from being thrown back onto the beach.

Amazingly, the hatchlings swim continuously for up to twenty-four hours after entering the water. This "swim frenzy" gets them into deeper water and away from predators prowling the shallow water near the beach. After this frenetic beginning, they embark on what is called their "lost year," a period of time that may actually range from one to several years in which they are rarely observed and no one is positive where they go or what they do. By the time they are seen again, they are juveniles and have grown considerably in length and weight.

As you can see, various species of sea turtle share many characteristics and behaviors through all phases of their life history. The following chapter will highlight differences among species and focus on some of the most fascinating aspects of each species of sea turtle.

An immature loggerhead turtle swims near the surface in the Gulf Stream. Once a hatchling leaves its natal beach, it swims nonstop for up to twenty-four hours until it reaches the relative safety of sargassum weeds or other flotsam caught in convergence zones of surface currents. This pelagic phase of the sea turtle's life, also known as its "lost year," may in fact last one to several years. (Photo © Doug Perrine/Innerspace Visions–Miami)

The Sea Turtles of the World

There are currently eight recognized living species of sea turtles grouped into six genera. Genus *Caretta* consists of the loggerhead (*Caretta caretta*). Genus *Lepidochelys*, the ridleys, has two members—the Kemp's ridley (*Lepidochelys kempi*) and the olive ridley (*Lepidochelys olivacea*). Genus *Eretmochelys* is represented by the hawksbill (*Eretmochelys imbricata*), genus *Dermchelys* by the leatherback (*Dermochelys coriacea*), and genus *Natator* by the Australian flatback (*Natator depressus*). Genus *Chelonia* includes the green turtle (*Chelonia mydas*) and the black turtle (*Chelonia agassizi*), until recently considered a subspecies of the green.

There is considerable debate regarding the validity of classifying the black turtle as a distinct species. Morphologically, its steep carapace and dark pigmentation make it quite different from the green turtle. Recent findings from mitochondrial DNA analysis, however, suggest that there is little genetic difference between the two animals, regardless of appearance. Although the black turtle is designated as a separate species as of this writing, it will be discussed with the green turtle because of its possible return to subspecies status and because of the clouded distinction between it and the green turtle in the Pacific. Earlier in this century, the Australian flatback faced similar taxonomic controversy, but after careful anatomical study by scientists, it was moved from genus *Chelonia* and is now accepted as the sole representative of Genus *Natator*.

Loggerhead (*Caretta caretta*)

The loggerhead is a large, yellow and reddish brown turtle named for its exceptionally large head. A hatchling is about two inches (5 cm) long and will grow into an adult weighing 200 to 350 pounds (91–159 kg) and measuring thirty-three to forty inches (84–102 cm) in carapace length. The head of an adult, which seems enormous in proportion to the rest of the turtle, may be as much as ten inches (25 cm) wide and is packed with powerful jaw muscles, which allow the turtle to crush the heavy-shelled clams, crustaceans, and encrusting animals (creatures often attached to rocks and reefs) that make up the bulk of its prey. The carapace is extremely thick toward the rear, which may provide this relatively slow swimmer with added protection against sharks. Biologists estimate that a loggerhead reaches maturity between twelve and thirty years of age.

A green sea turtle in deep, clear, blue water off the Hawaiian Islands.
(Photo © Doug Perrine/Innerspace Visions—Miami)

A diver discovers a sleeping loggerhead turtle on a shipwreck off Grand Bahama Island, Bahamas. Sea turtles can rest or sleep underwater for several hours at a time. (Photo © Doug Perrine/Innerspace Visions—Miami)

Its flippers a blur, a hatchling loggerhead turtle scrambles frantically through the sand toward the ocean at Cape Lookout National Seashore, North Carolina. (Photo © Connie Toops)

A closeup of the head and front flippers of a loggerhead turtle. The loggerhead is named for its exceptionally large head, which seems enormous in proportion to the rest of its body. (Photo © Doug Perrine/ Innerspace Visions—Miami)

Loggerheads are found in temperate and subtropical coastal waters throughout much of the world. Adults rarely stray far from mainland shores, preferring to feed in estuaries and in the relatively shallow water along the continental shelves of the Atlantic, Pacific, and Indian Oceans. In the Western Hemisphere, they range as far north as Newfoundland and as far south as Argentina. In some areas, loggerheads congregate to take advantage of locally abundant food sources. Thousands of juvenile loggerheads forage on horseshoe crabs during the summer in the mouths of rivers emptying into Chesapeake Bay on the mid-Atlantic coast of the United States, as well as in the deeper channels of the bay. An estimated ten thousand juvenile loggerheads congregate off the Baja California coast to feed on massive concentrations of pelagic red crabs.

Loggerheads nest in the subtropics and the north and south temperate zones, generally avoiding the tropical beaches favored by other species in Central America, northern South America, and the Old World. They also apparently don't nest on islands in the central and western Pacific. The most important nesting grounds for loggerheads are in the Middle East on Masirah Island, Oman, and on several scattered barrier island beaches along the coast of the southeastern United States. Masirah Island's annual nesting population is approximately thirty thousand females, while up to twenty-five thousand loggerheads nest in the southeastern United States each year. The bulk of nesting in the United States, numbering as many as fourteen thousand nests, takes place along the east coast of Florida between the inlet at Cape Canaveral south to Sebastian Inlet.

Female loggerheads that nest in Florida mate during a single receptive period from March through June. Males do not stay with the females for the entire nesting season; instead, most males will depart for their foraging grounds by the middle of June, while most females leave by September. The distance from nesting beaches to feeding grounds can range from a few hundred miles to more than a thousand miles. For example, loggerheads that nest on Florida beaches may disperse as far north as New Jersey and range south to the Bahamas, the Florida Keys, Cuba, the Dominican Republic, and into the Gulf of Mexico.

Hawksbill (*Eretmochelys imbricata*)

The hawksbill is a relatively small sea turtle, measuring thirty to thirty-six inches (76–91 cm) in carapace length and weighing 89 to 133 pounds (40–60 kg). It is easily identified by its narrow head and strongly hooked beak, as well as by its distinctive carapace. The carapace is dark amber in color with radiating streaks of brown or black, strongly serrated along the posterior edge, and covered by thick, overlapping scales. For

The hawksbill turtle is among the few vertebrates in the world that dine almost exclusively on sponges. This hawksbill is feeding on sponges over a reef off Palm Beach, Florida. (Photo © Doug Perrine/ Innerspace Visions–Miami)

A hawksbill turtle swims over a coral crest in the Andaman Sea off Thailand. (Photo © Doug Perrine/Innerspace Visions–Miami)

centuries, the hawksbill was hunted for its beautiful shell—the source of natural tortoiseshell—as well as for its eggs. Hawksbill populations dropped dramatically under the intense exploitation. With adequate protection, the turtle might make a comeback.

Hawksbills are considered the most tropical of the sea turtles, favoring the clear, relatively shallow water of coastal reefs, bays, estuaries, and lagoons found in the subtropical and tropical Atlantic, Pacific, and Indian Oceans. They are seen regularly off the Atlantic coast of Florida, in the Bahamas and Florida Keys, and in the Gulf of Mexico. Adults tend to stay in deeper water than juveniles, foraging in depths up to 330 feet (100 m). Juveniles generally stay close to shallow reefs at depths less than 66 feet (20 m).

The diet of the hawksbill is one of its most fascinating aspects. These turtles are among the few vertebrates that specialize in feeding on sponges. Some sponges are toxic to certain marine creatures and are generally considered unpalatable by many others, mainly because of the tiny, siliceous (glasslike) spicules in the skin. These spicules make up a large percentage of the mass of a sponge. Other spongivores (sponge-eaters) have morphological adaptations that enable them to handle the spicules more easily, but nothing similar has been found in hawksbills. Spicules are found imbedded in the intestines of hawksbills, but do not seem to have harmed the animals. How hawksbills handle the spicules or survive the toxins produced by some sponges in their diet is still not fully understood.

Hawksbills prefer to nest alone or in small groups on isolated beaches of tropical islands or sparsely inhabited continental shores around the world. Their mode of nesting, called "dispersed nesting" by biologists, may be an important reason why there are any hawksbills left at all. Because hawksbills scatter their nests along long stretches of isolated beaches rather than concentrating in dense rookeries, poachers have been unable to systematically plunder eggs and kill females on shore. Although hawksbills sometimes nest in the company of green turtles or other species, their small size allows them to climb over reefs, rocks, and debris to nest among the roots of vegetation on beaches, areas that are not as accessible to larger, less-agile sea turtles.

Hawksbills nesting on islands in the eastern Caribbean lay approximately five separate nests per season on a two- to three-year cycle. A clutch averages 150 eggs, although one female was documented laying 215 eggs. Hatchlings are light to dark brown and, like most other turtles, embark on a pelagic voyage that may last several years. When the juveniles are about ten inches long, they travel to coastal waters to become benthic (bottom) feeders on shallow coral reefs. They will eventually gravitate toward deeper reefs as they grow larger and become more capable of making deep dives for sponges.

Leatherback (*Dermochelys coriacea*)

The leatherback, or leathery turtle as it is sometimes called, is the champion among sea turtles. It grows larger, dives deeper, travels farther, and frequents colder water than any other sea turtle. Some aspects of its physiology and nesting behavior are strikingly different from other sea turtles' as well.

An adult leatherback is an enormous animal, averaging nearly eight hundred pounds (360 kg) in weight and sixty-four inches (160 cm) in carapace length throughout much of its range. However, eastern Pacific specimens are considerably smaller than those in the Atlantic and Indian Oceans. Few Pacific leatherbacks weigh more than 660 pounds (300 kg), which is still large by sea turtle standards. The largest leatherback ever recorded measured almost ten feet (3 m) from the tip of the beak across the curve of the shell to the tip of the tail.

Leatherbacks are named for their large, elongate shell, which, unlike the hard shells of other sea turtles, is composed of a thick layer of oily, cartilaginous material strengthened by thousands of tiny bones. Seven narrow ridges extend the length of the carapace. Although some ridges are characteristic of nearly all sea turtle hatchlings, the leatherback is the only species to retain them to adulthood. The carapace, head, and flippers are typically black with many white spots. The soft plastron is also ridged and is white with dark blotches. Leatherback coloration—dark above and light below—is characteristic of many pelagic creatures, including the hatchlings of several other sea turtle species. The ridges along the back are thought to act as keels, and the smooth transition between the head, flippers, and shell may help these turtles to cut through the water more efficiently. Unlike other sea turtles, adult leatherbacks have no scales and no claws on their flippers.

Hatchling leatherbacks are two and one-half inches (6.25 cm) long and dark gray to black with a white border on the flippers and white stripes along the ridges of the carapace. Within a short time the white striping and borders give way to the random spots of the adults. Small scales cover both the carapace and flippers of hatchlings, but these too disappear within a couple of months after birth. The foreflippers of hatchlings are as long as the shell and may attain a length of thirty-nine inches (1 m) by the time the turtles reach adulthood.

Leatherbacks are the most widely distributed of the sea turtles. Their travels take them from nesting

beaches in the tropical Atlantic, Pacific, and Indian Oceans to feeding grounds in temperate waters as far north as Canada, Iceland, and Norway in the Atlantic Ocean, and as far south as New Zealand and Chile in the Pacific. The migrations to feeding grounds often involve journeys of more than 3,100 miles (5,000 km) from their nesting beaches. Recent studies indicate the turtles may use established migratory routes along continental shelves that follow deepwater bathymetric contours, or fluctuations in water depth. These contours create a steeply sloping sea bottom ranging in depth from 660 feet to nearly 5,000 feet (200–1,500 m). Why these narrow travel corridors are significant to the leatherbacks is not yet understood, although food availability, the turtles' physiological capabilities, and the use of the bottom structure for navigational purposes may be factors.

Nesting season finds leatherbacks laying their eggs in colonies ranging from twenty-five to six thousand females on tropical mainland beaches or large islands, especially those with a deep-water approach, heavy surf, and a steep, sandy slope up to the storm tide zone. This topography shortens the distance the turtle must travel over the beach to reach dry sand above the high-tide mark. They stay away from rocky areas or coral reefs, which would damage the soft, unprotected plastron. Even a crawl up a sandy beach can be enough to scrape the turtle's skin and cause bleeding. They also avoid extensive mudflats, which they find difficult to traverse.

The major leatherback rookeries in the world include the northern coast of South America, especially at Silebache, French Guiana; and in Mexico along the coastal areas near Michoacan, Guerrero, and Oaxaca. Moderately large populations nest on Trinidad; at Bigisanti, Surinam; and near Matina on the Caribbean coast of Costa Rica. Some low-density nesting (twenty to thirty nests annually) occurs outside the tropics in Florida and in South Africa. Estimates on the number of breeding females worldwide range from about 70,000 to 115,000.

Studies in the U.S. Virgin Islands show that leatherbacks begin nesting within a week of arriving from temperate latitudes. Mating must take place before or during migration to the nesting beaches because there is not enough time for the females to copulate and develop eggs off the nesting beach. Leatherbacks have the shortest renesting interval of all sea turtles, returning to lay eggs every nine to ten days during the nesting season for a total of four to ten times. Records for some beaches indicate that leatherbacks return to nest at

A leatherback turtle swims through the clear, blue waters of the open Pacific. Leatherbacks are the largest and most pelagic of the sea turtles. (Photo © Doug Perrine/Innerspace Visions–Miami)

During the nesting season, a leatherback turtle may return to the beach to renest every nine or ten days. This leatherback is finishing her nest on a dark beach in Mexico. (Photo © Doug Perrine/Innerspace Visions—Miami)

two- to three-year intervals.

Leatherbacks rarely make false nesting emergences as is commonly seen with green turtles or logger-heads, and unless they are disturbed by predators, they proceed methodically through the nesting process. They drag themselves up the beach with simultaneous movements of their huge front flippers, leaving an impressive track that may stretch more than six feet (2 m) wide. The return track to the sea is distinctive as well and may include one or more circular loops that are the result of several tightly maneuvered turns by the female as she attempted to orient herself toward the sea by searching for the lightest area on the horizon. Some leatherback hatchlings also perform these orientation circles, while others scramble without hesitation toward the sea. Leatherbacks are strongly attracted to light and can easily get directed away from the ocean—an important reason to prevent the lights of oceanfront development from shining on the beach during the nesting season.

Leatherback hatchlings erupt from a nest at dawn, Michoacan, Mexico. Such daytime emergences are risky because of the baby turtles' increased exposure to predators, particularly birds. (Photo © George H. H. Huey)

A leatherback nest is unusual in several respects. First, the nest cavity is much deeper than other sea turtle nests due to the longer reach of a leatherback's large back flippers. Second, because of the great depth of the nest chamber, which may be buried under more than two feet of sand, incubation averages sixty-five to seventy days—somewhat longer than the time required to incubate eggs of sea turtles with shallower nests. Third, a leatherback female spends more time and effort than other sea turtles disguising the exact location of the egg chamber at the nest site. She may also build several false body pits several feet away from the actual nest site, moving hundreds of pounds of sand in the process. In all, a female leatherback may spend more than thirty minutes in nest concealment alone.

The average clutch of an Atlantic leatherback contains between eighty and ninety normal-sized eggs, each more than two inches (5–6 cm) in diameter. In the eastern Pacific, fewer than sixty eggs are typically laid per clutch. Unlike other sea turtles, leatherbacks lay several undersized, yolkless eggs in addition to the normal-sized, fertile eggs. The infertile eggs are the last to be deposited in the egg chamber, and the number varies in each clutch. No one is certain why the females lay these "duds." One theory is that because leatherback eggs are so large, there is a danger that sand will fall into the narrow spaces between the eggs and impair gas exchange. By dropping a large number of small eggs on top of the clutch, a "cap" is placed on the nest that fills the spaces and reduces the chances of this happening.

Leatherbacks feed almost exclusively on coelenterates, especially jellyfish. Their jaws are scissorlike and deeply notched in front, obviously adapted for holding and cutting slippery prey. Flexible spines in the mouth cavity and throat are directed toward the stomach so that food is retained when water taken in with the prey is expelled. It is a mystery how leatherbacks manage to grow to such a large size considering their diet of watery, nutrient-poor organisms, although hatchlings in captivity can consume up to twice their weight in jellyfish every day.

The pursuit of jellyfish often requires leatherbacks to endure cold water temperatures during deep dives and when migrating to temperate regions. Leatherbacks have overcome this problem by becoming one of the few reptiles that can modulate their internal body temperature. Active leatherbacks have been reported at water temperatures below 43°F (6°C); no other reptile is known to remain active at this temperature. Body temperature for a leatherback can range from as little as 5°F (3° C) above ambient water temperature to more than 32°F (18°C). How do they do it? Sheer mass helps. Their tremendous bulk enables them to conserve more heat than could a smaller body. Oily, fibrous tissue in the shell acts as insulation against the cold. However, the most important factor in their endothermic capabilities is probably a highly efficient countercurrent heat exchange mechanism in the circulatory system of their long flippers.

Leatherbacks are also renowned for their phenomenal diving ability. Dr. Scott Eckert and his colleagues reported that post-nesting females equipped with depth recorders dove to depths of more than 3,300 feet (1,000 m), an achievement unparalleled by any other air-breathing animal with the exception of sperm whales and elephant seals. The shallowest dives occurred at dusk and the deepest at dawn, possibly because they were feeding on jellyfish that concentrate below 2,000 feet (600 m) during the day and move toward the surface at night. Leatherbacks can attain these great depths in part because they lack a rigid breastbone or lower chest (skeletal features found in all other sea turtles), adaptations that allow the chest to collapse during deep dives. Furthermore, the prodigious quantities of oil in the skin and shell absorb nitrogen and help to prevent decompression problems during diving and resurfacing.

Kemp's ridley (*Lepidochelys kempi*)

The ridleys are the smallest of the sea turtles. The Kemp's ridley is slightly larger than the olive ridley, measuring twenty-four to twenty-eight inches (62–70 cm) in carapace length and weighing seventy-eight to one hundred pounds (35–45 kg) when mature. An adult is olive green above and yellowish below, with a large head and powerful jaws. The carapace is circular to heart-shaped. Hatchlings are dark gray and just over one and one-half inches (44 mm) long.

Although the Kemp's ridley was first described by Samuel Garman in 1880, this turtle was not recognized as a distinct species until the 1940s. It was frequently confused with its closest relative, the olive ridley, and with the loggerhead. However, confusion about Kemp's ridleys continued into the 1950s, with many herpetologists convinced the creature was a sterile hybrid between the green and loggerhead. No one could locate the nesting beaches, no one could find the turtles massed together for breeding, and no one had ever captured an egg-bearing female. It was not until 1963 when an old film made in 1947 by Mexican engineer Andrés Herrera was rediscovered that the location of the nesting beach of the Kemp's ridleys became known to biologists. The film showed what was eventually estimated to be forty thousand Kemp's ridleys coming ashore to nest on an isolated strip of beach now called Rancho Nuevo in the state of Tamaulipas, Mexico, approximately two hundred miles (300 km) south of Brownsville, Texas. So many turtles were nesting at once that they were climbing over each other and unearthing each other's eggs as they dug out their own nests. The faded, flickering Kodachrome images of thousands of ridleys nesting on the Mexican shoreline astounded herpetologists everywhere. As Archie Carr effused in *The Sea Turtle—So Excellent a Fishe*, the film was "the cinema of the year . . . the picture of the decade . . . the movie of all time." For the late Dr. Carr and other researchers who had spent years puzzling over the ridleys, it provided a "reverberating answer to a twenty-year-old question." Biologists subsequently searched for other nesting beaches throughout the world but discovered no other significant locations. Ninety-five percent of the population comes to the seventeen-

A Kemp's ridley prepares to nest at Rancho Nuevo, Mexico. Ninety-five percent of all Kemp's ridleys nest on this seventeen-mile strip of beach. (Photo © Carlos Hernandez)

mile strip of beach at Rancho Nuevo, with the remaining five percent nesting in the adjacent state of Veracruz. No other sea turtle species relies almost entirely on a single breeding site.

The mass emergence, or *arribada* (Spanish for "arrival"), of Kemp's ridleys at Rancho Nuevo occurs at irregular intervals between April and June. Arribadas may be repeated several times over a season, and some females may nest in successive seasons. Male and female ridleys congregate off the beaches to mate, perhaps using cues such as wind direction or velocity, lunar cycles, or water temperature to determine when to gather. Once they have mated, the females wait for several days for conditions to be just right to come ashore. These conditions generally include a high northeast wind and heavy surf, with the arribada occurring during daylight. The high wind serves to erase traces of the nests and hide them from predators, as well as to keep the females from overheating during the strenuous ordeal. Mass nestings are thought to serve as a type of predator "swamping" in which some nesting females and hatchlings will be lost, but many more will survive. Predators seem to know when an arribada will occur, because coyotes and vultures move from inland areas to the beach before the turtles arrive.

Herrera's film not only revealed the grandeur of the arribada, but also provided a baseline against which to measure the disheartening decline of the Kemp's ridley since 1947. The forty thousand turtles on the beach in 1947 had dwindled to two thousand by 1966. That year, the Mexican government set up its first camp to monitor the beach and protect the turtles from *hueveros,* or egg takers. Prior to the 1960s, thousands of females were captured offshore and cut open just for their eggs, and hundreds of thousands of eggs were transported by mule train over the mountains to market. In 1977, Rancho Nuevo was declared a Natural Reserve by Mexico, and programs were instituted to protect the nesting beach and reduce poaching and the natural mortality of eggs. Eggs are moved to protective enclosures to decrease the loss to predators, and some 50,000 hatchlings are released on the beach each year. In spite of these programs, estimates from nest counts in 1993 placed the number of adult females at about four hundred. The reduction in numbers has resulted in the fragmentation of the arribadas into small groups and solitary nestings. The remaining females lay fewer than one thousand nests each season. The effects of the past plundering of nest sites and continued high death tolls in shrimp nets are the principal culprits pushing the Kemp's ridley to its current status as the most endangered of the sea turtles.

The range of the Kemp's ridley is limited for the most part to the Gulf of Mexico, where adults forage in productive coastal and estuarine waters, particularly along the Louisiana coast near the mouth of the Mississippi River and in the Campeche, Mexico, region. Because Kemp's ridleys feed primarily on crabs that share the habitat of white, pink, and brown *Penaeus* shrimp, it is no accident that the turtles are common bycatch in shrimp nets in those places. Crabs of the family Portunidae, such as blue crabs, are favorite prey, but clams, mussels, and snails are also eaten.

A tagged Kemp's ridley nesting at Rancho Nuevo, Mexico. Unlike other sea turtles, Kemp's ridleys nest almost exclusively during the day.
(Photo © Peter C. H. Pritchard)

Like most other sea turtles, Kemp's ridleys embark on a pelagic phase after hatching. As young Kemp's ridleys near maturity, they move to either a permanent feeding ground or a series of feeding grounds among which they routinely travel. Juvenile Kemp's ridleys are found off Cedar Key on the northwest coast of Florida and elsewhere in the Gulf of Mexico from Texas to Florida. In addition, a contingent of juvenile turtles is regularly seen in several places along the eastern seaboard as far north as Cape Cod, Massachusetts. Kemp's ridleys are occasionally caught in shrimp trawls that operate in the area around Cape Canaveral, Florida. However, in cooperation with biologists, some shrimpers tag and release many. The Kemp's ridley is the most common species of marine turtle recorded at the Wellfleet Bay Wildlife Sanctuary on Cape Cod. Furthermore, there are several published records of Kemp's ridleys in Long Island Sound, including a total of forty-four juveniles (most of them cold-stunned) that washed up along the eastern two-thirds of Long Island's north shore between December 1985 and March 1986.

There has been considerable controversy over how this "lost" east coast population fits into the overall distribution of Kemp's ridleys. Do they move into northern waters to feed during the summer and then retreat to southern waters during the winter, as do loggerheads that nest on the southeastern coast of the United States? Or are they, as some researchers suggest, merely "waifs" that never return to the Gulf of

An olive ridley arribada at Ostional, Costa Rica. While the once vast Kemp's ridley arribadas have been reduced to small groups or solitary nestings, olive ridleys still congregate on a few beaches in arribadas that number between 5,000 and 150,000 females. (Photo © Peter C. H. Pritchard)

Mexico and Rancho Nuevo? The great distance and contrary currents make such a southerly journey difficult. Furthermore, during this trek, the turtles would probably pass through the Bahamas or the Greater and Lesser Antilles, but no one has ever seen a Kemp's ridley in the Caribbean. Only one turtle tagged near Cape Canaveral has ever been recaptured. Kemp's ridleys are found in the Florida Straits and in the Florida Keys, but it is entirely possible that these are turtles that have never left the Gulf of Mexico. The question of the "lost" ridleys is only one of the many riddles that remain unanswered about this enigmatic, critically endangered species.

An olive ridley returns to sea after nesting at Mexiquillo Beach, on the Pacific coast of Mexico. (Photo © Doug Perrine/Innerspace Visions–Miami)

Olive ridley (*Lepidochelys olivacea*)

The Nahuatl Indians of Mexico call the olive ridley *Chiwanini*, meaning "little one," and indeed this species is the smallest of the sea turtles. Adults typically weigh less than one hundred pounds (35–40 kg) and measure only twenty-two to thirty inches (55–75 cm) in carapace length. The turtle's common name, olive ridley, derives from the olive green, heart-shaped carapace of the adult. The plastron is yellowish. Hatchlings are dark gray overall, developing pale undersides as they grow older, and measure one to one-and-one-half inches (25–40 mm) at birth.

Olive ridleys are widespread throughout the tropical waters of the northern Indian Ocean, the Atlantic Ocean, and along the eastern edge of the Pacific Ocean. They are currently considered the least threatened of the sea turtles, but as with other species, their numbers are dwindling. Shrimp trawlers catch tens of thousands of olive ridleys each year off the Pacific coast of Central America and the Indian state of Orissa in the Bay of Bengal. The ongoing illegal harvest of eggs and the killing of adult turtles by commercial fishermen have virtually eliminated olive ridley nesting at several sites in Mexico, and olive ridley populations in both Surinam and India are near collapse.

Most major olive ridley rookeries are found on mainland shores near the mouths of rivers or estuaries, typically in areas of high turbidity and low salinity. They nest singly or in small groups, as well as in arribadas, like the Kemp's ridley. Olive ridleys rarely nest on small oceanic islands, although there are a few nesting populations on large islands near continents, such as Madagascar and Sri Lanka in the Indian Ocean. Currently, the most important colonies include one beach in Mexico, three sites in India, two areas in Costa Rica, and two beaches in Nicaragua. It is at these beaches that the olive ridleys congregate to nest over the course of several nights in arribadas that may number between 5,000 and 150,000 females.

Unlike the Kemp's ridleys in Mexico, olive ridleys nest throughout the year in Central America. At Playa Nancite, Costa Rica, biologists have recorded arribadas in every month, although peak nesting is from August to December. Arribadas that occur during the January to April dry season, as well as during the first couple months of the wet season, are generally smaller and last fewer nights than the great arrivals of the peak nesting season. More than 75 percent of the arribadas start within a few days of the first and last quarter moons—the times of neap tides, which are the lowest high tides of the month. As with the arribadas of Kemp's ridleys in Mexico and olive ridleys in Surinam, strong winds may help stimulate daytime arribadas of the olive ridleys in Costa Rica.

Olive ridleys nest on an annual cycle that is periodically interrupted by one or more years away from the nesting beach. Females lay two clutches per season at intervals of approximately twenty-eight to thirty days. Each clutch contains about one hundred eggs. It takes an olive ridley female an average of fifty minutes to nest—the fastest nesting time for sea turtles. After the eggs incubate in the sand for forty-five to sixty-five days, the nestlings emerge and scramble down to the water's edge to head out to sea.

After adult olive ridleys leave the nesting beaches, they typically embark on migrations to distant feeding areas. Not much is known about their distribution from specific nesting sites, but tag returns from Costa Rican olive ridleys nesting at Nancite and Ostional indicate that many ridleys embark on long migrations to feeding areas in the eastern Pacific Ocean from Mexico to Peru. One was even found nearly 1,500 miles (2,400 km) west of Costa Rica.

Olive ridleys frequently forage far offshore, diving to depths of 500 feet (150 m) or more in search of bottom-dwelling shrimp, crabs, snails, tunicates, sea urchins, and other invertebrates. They also spend a considerable amount of time at the surface over areas of deep ocean, where they may feed on jellyfish and other organisms that undertake nightly migrations from the ocean depths.

A green turtle swims with a remora over a Malaysian reef. Green turtles get their name from their greenish body fat, not from their overall color. Coloration in green turtles varies from greenish or brown to black or gray, with dark markings on the carapace. (Photo © Burt Jones/Maurine Shimlock—Secret Sea Visions™)

Green turtle (*Chelonia mydas*) and black turtle (*Chelonia agassizi*)

The green turtle is probably the best known sea turtle because of its historic food value and the amount of research that has been conducted on behalf of its preservation. Its name comes not from its external color, but from the greenish color of the fat. Its meat is a highly regarded food, and cartilage from the plastron, called *calipee*, is scraped from slaughtered turtles to provide the base for green turtle soup—a centuries-old delicacy. The smooth carapace of an adult varies in color from greenish or brown to black or gray, frequently marked with darker streaks and spots. The bottom of the carapace is white or yellowish. In adult females, the tail barely reaches the edge of the carapace; in adult males, the tail is much longer, extending well beyond the edge of the carapace. The tail of an adult male is tipped with a very flat nail, which, together with a large, single, curved claw on each foreflipper, helps the male grasp the female during mating. The rounded head of a green turtle seems small compared to the rest of the body and is easily distinguished from other sea turtles' by the single pair of scales in front of the eyes. The lower jaw is serrated, perhaps an adaptation that allows it to more easily tear sea grass, an important food.

A green turtle raises its head to breathe near the Cayman Islands in the Caribbean Sea. Sea turtles need only one to three seconds on the surface to catch their breath. (Photo © Doug Perrine/Innerspace Visions—Miami)

The green turtle is the largest of the Cheloniidae. It is a circumtropical species that ranges throughout the warmer areas of the Atlantic, Pacific, and Indian Oceans, as well as in the Mediterranean Sea. Populations around the world vary in their average length and weight, with the turtles in the Atlantic and Caribbean being the largest. Nesting females in Florida average 3.3 feet (101.5 cm) in carapace length and 303 pounds (136.2 kg) in weight. Green turtles in the eastern Pacific and black turtles are somewhat smaller, averaging thirty-two inches (80 cm) in carapace length and 144 to 278 pounds (65–125 kg) in weight. Pacific green turtles vary widely in color, ranging from the normal olive color to the melanistic black turtle (known as *tortuga negra* in the Galápagos) to individuals that are nearly white (*tortuga blanca* in Peru). A rare yellow form, possibly large immatures from the French Polynesia nesting population, occurs in the Galápagos and is known locally as *tortuga amarilla*. Hatchlings of all green turtles are about the size of a half dollar (50 mm)—dark-colored above and white below. Black turtles are similar to green turtles in all respects except for their somewhat steeper carapace and overall gray to black coloration.

As with most other sea turtles, hatchling greens embark on a pelagic phase from their natal beach that may last several years. During this time, they are carnivores, feeding on jellyfish, small mollusks, crustaceans, sponges, and other tiny creatures sharing the refuge offered by flotsam or sargassum caught in the convergence zones of offshore surface currents. When they attain a carapace length of eight to ten inches (20–25 cm), they turn to a predominately vegetarian diet, which they will keep throughout their adult lives, and move to nearshore feeding grounds. Algae and seagrasses are the most common food for adult green turtles, although they also consume mangrove leaves and occasionally hydrozoans. As adults, they typically forage over broad expanses of shallow, sandy flats covered with seagrasses or algae. Coral reefs, worm reefs, and rocky bottoms may also be used for feeding, especially when sea grass meadows are not present. Coral heads and large rocks near feeding grounds become handy sleeping shelters. Each turtle returns to the same sleeping shelter in the evening, even though the feeding area may be several miles away.

Important feeding grounds for green turtles include the Miskito Cays of Nicaragua, the coastal shallows of Brazil, the Gulf of Oman in the Middle East, the Arafura and Coral Seas between Vanuatu and Fiji in the South Pacific, the Pacific side of the Japanese Archipelago and the East China Sea, the coastal waters of Baja California, and the Pacific Coast of the Americas from Costa Rica to Peru.

Most green turtles migrate between their feeding areas and nesting beaches—journeys that can range from a few hundred to over one thousand miles. Some populations, however, such as the black turtles resident to the Galápagos and green turtles in Hawaii, complete their entire life cycle within a small geographic area. Others establish year-round residency during certain stages of the life cycle. For example, a population of immature green turtles is found year-round in the Indian River Lagoon system on Florida's east coast.

Green turtles in the wild grow slowly and do not mature until they are fifteen to fifty years of age, in part because their mainly vegetarian diet is low in protein and vitamin D. To partially offset this dietary imbalance, green turtles feeding on sea grasses sometimes maintain "grazing plots" by repeatedly trimming older vegeta-

This green turtle seems to fly as it swims over a bed of seagrass in the Florida Keys. Immature green turtles are carnivorous, feeding on jellyfish and other small ocean creatures, but as they mature, they become vegetarians and depend on seagrasses and algae for sustenance. (Photo © Bill Keogh)

tive growth within the plot. The trimming promotes new plant growth, which is higher in protein and lower in fiber than older leaves. Consuming the new growth allows the turtles to boost their protein intake. To compensate for the lack of vitamin D in the diet, green turtles often bask, either by lingering for long periods at the surface of the water or by completely hauling themselves out on the beach. Beach basking is particularly prevalent in the northwestern Hawaiian Islands, in Australia, and in the Galápagos Islands. To prevent overheating, beach basking usually takes place on white sand with a steady wind and partly cloudy conditions. Basking is also thought to accelerate the development of eggs in females and reduce the interval between nestings, especially since most of the basking (at least in the Hawaiian Islands) takes place during the nesting season.

Major rookeries for green turtles include Tortuguero, Costa Rica, and Aves Island in the Caribbean Sea; Surinam and Ascension Island in the south Atlantic Ocean; Oman in the Middle East; the Seychelles Islands in the Indian Ocean; and the Hawaiian Islands, Philippine Islands, and Michoacan, Mexico, in the Pacific. However, the largest populations are found in Australia. Green turtles also nest in significant numbers along the east coast of Florida, particularly in Brevard, Indian River, St. Lucie, Martin, Palm Beach, and Broward Counties. A small population nests at Lara Bay on the Akamas Peninsula of Cyprus, and these turtles may complete their entire life cycle within the Mediterranean Sea. Black turtles are the only sea turtles known to nest on the Galápagos Islands.

Green turtles mate in the water, often offshore from their nesting beaches. The females come ashore at night to deposit up to eight or nine clutches per breeding season at intervals of twelve to fourteen days. The number of eggs in each clutch averages 110 to 115 ping-pong-ball–sized eggs, and the entire nesting process takes approximately two hours. Like most other sea turtles, green turtles disguise the nest. Females generally nest on a two- to five-year cycle, but males may migrate from their feeding grounds every year to mate. The incubation period for green turtle eggs averages fifty-five to sixty days.

Green turtles in some areas are afflicted by tumorlike growths called fibropapillomas. The growths cover the eyes of the turtles with masses of diseased tissue, hindering their ability to find food and increasing their susceptibility to becoming entangled in debris. Fibropapillomas were first found on green turtles from the Florida Keys in 1938, but the disease is now widespread and attacks males and females ranging in size from twelve-inch (30-cm) juveniles to full-size adults. The juveniles seem to be affected more so than adults.

A male black turtle in the Galápagos Islands. An adult male sea turtle can usually be distinguished from an adult female by the long tail that extends beyond the carapace and by the strongly curved claw on the leading edge of each foreflipper. (Photo © Doug Perrine/Innerspace Visions—Miami)

A black turtle rests on a ledge in the Galápagos. Black turtles, considered by many scientists to be an eastern Pacific subspecies of the green turtle, are the only sea turtles known to nest in the Galápagos. (Photo © Marilyn Kazmers/SharkSong)

Although the cause is unknown, fibropapillomas may be stimulated by external parasites, high water temperatures, excessive solar radiation, and pollution. Increasing numbers of loggerheads and olive ridleys are showing up with papillomalike maladies as well.

Australian flatback (*Natator depressus*)

Considered by taxonomists to be one of the most primitive members of the Cheloniidae, the Australian flatback is an intriguing creature whose life history contradicts many general assumptions regarding sea turtles. It is not a wide-ranging species like other sea turtles. Instead, its range is limited to the coastal waters of Australia. In addition, it produces only half the average number of eggs per clutch as other sea turtles, and its large hatchlings do not embark on a pelagic voyage as part of their life cycle. Morphologically, the Australian flatback's closest relatives appear to be the ridleys, although it exhibits many similarities to the green turtle and until recently was grouped with that species in genus *Chelonia*.

The Australian flatback was first described as a new species (*Chelonia depressa*) in 1880 by Samuel Garman from two specimens—one a stuffed adult male from Harvard's Museum of Comparative Zoology and the other a juvenile. G. Baur in 1890 thought the flatback differed enough from other sea turtles to possibly warrant its own genus, and A. R. McCulloch followed this line of thought in 1908 with a formal proposal renaming the turtle *Natator tesselatus*. This new description was not accepted by other herpetologists, and *Chelonia depressa* remained the formal species name throughout much of the twentieth century. Some herpetologists were skeptical even of the flatback's individual species status, claiming that there was not enough comparative evidence available to make a distinction between it and the green turtle. At the time, most museum collections had few specimens of Australian flatbacks, and most of these were young individuals.

However, photographs in the late 1960s comparing the external characteristics of green turtles against those of Australian flatbacks demonstrated enough variation between the two species to spark renewed effort to revive the generic name (*Natator*). The careful study of four complete adult skeletons at the Bishop Museum in Honolulu, Hawaii, in the 1980s left no doubt that the Australian flatback was quite different from every other sea turtle, and the combination *Natator depressus* was adopted.

The Australian flatback is a medium-sized turtle, measuring thirty to thirty-eight inches (76–96 cm) in carapace length and weighing an average of 156 pounds (70 kg). Adult females are larger than adult males, but have short tails in contrast to the much longer tails of the males. Both have relatively short flippers and a broad head. The head and neck are olive-gray above and cream colored below. The flattened carapace, from which the common name "flatback" is derived, is olive-gray in color, oval in shape, noticeably upturned at the edges, and greasy to the touch.

One unusual characteristic of this sea turtle is the thinness of the keratin covering the carapace and flippers. The keratin is so thin that a thumbnail run firmly across the top of the shell will draw blood. If the turtle is flipped on its back, the slapping of its flippers against its plastron often causes bleeding from the tips of the flippers and bruises under the keratin of the plastron.

Australian flatbacks prefer shallow, turbid, inshore waters and bays, where they feed on sea cucumbers and other holothurians, as well as jellyfish, prawns, mollusks, bryozoans, and other invertebrates. There are no records of flatbacks from clear-water coral reef habitats where other sea turtles are often found. The range of this species encompasses the broad, gently sloping continental shelf of northwest and northern Australia to the lagoon environment shoreward of eastern Australia's Great Barrier Reef. The

Four Australian flatback hatchlings scramble toward the surf. The Australian flatback is the only sea turtle that does not have a pelagic phase in its life cycle. (Photo © Peter C. H. Pritchard)

only records of Australian flatbacks outside of Australian territorial waters comes from shrimp trawl bycatch in New Guinea's Gulf of Papua, just north of the continent. Their nesting range is predominantly tropical, extending from northwestern Australia eastward along the coast of Queensland. Queensland's most important rookery for the flatback is Crab Island, in the Gulf of Carpentaria, which supports year-round nesting for thousands of turtles. Other major rookeries are on Wild Duck and Avoid Islands, in-shore of the southern Great Barrier Reef, with low-density nesting occurring throughout the coastal areas of the Gulf of Carpentaria and the shallow coastal waters sheltered by the Great Barrier Reef. Nesting activity also occurs in the Sir Edward Pellew Islands.

Most nesting occurs in November and December, with mating occurring at that time in the shallow waters off the beaches. The females dig their nests in the early evening on the tops of sand dunes or on steep seaward slopes. The eggs are just over two inches (51 mm) in diameter, and the clutch size averages fifty-six

An Australian flatback heads toward the surf after laying her eggs on Crab Island, at the northern tip of Queensland, Australia. Note the upward-curved edge of the carapace, a distinguishing characteristic of this species. (Photo © Peter C. H. Pritchard)

eggs (compared with 100 to 150 for most species). The female lays up to four clutches each season. Incubation takes approximately six weeks, with hatchlings emerging in the cool of the night. The hatchlings are larger than most sea turtles of equivalent adult size, averaging more than two inches (60 mm) in carapace length. The large size of the hatchlings allows them to ward off attacks by crabs, gulls, egrets, and smaller fish that may feed on the nestlings of other sea turtles. They are stronger swimmers and have larger energy reserves than most other sea turtle hatchlings to prevent being swept away from nearshore waters by seaward currents. Hatchling flatbacks stay in nearshore water because there is no pelagic phase in their life cycle, unlike other sea turtles.

It seems that after the initial swim frenzy from the natal beaches, hatchling flatbacks seek out the shallow, turbid waters of the northern Australian coast, possibly wandering into mangrove areas. Researchers obtained evidence supporting this premise through studies of the remains of prey at feeding stations of white-bellied sea eagles (*Haliaeetus leucogaster*) in northern Australia. Sea eagles fish estuarine and nearshore waters of this region, snatching fish, sea snakes, and turtles from the water's surface. Of the remains of turtles, only small freshwater species and juvenile Australian flatbacks were found. Sea eagles rarely fish beyond the coastal shallows, and researchers recorded no other sea turtle juveniles from the remains of the sea eagles' meals. The evidence from the sea eagle feeding stations was strengthened by other researchers who reported seeing all growth stages of flatbacks in shallow bays in northern Australia, including two immature turtles with estimated carapace lengths of less than eight inches (20 cm). The absence of an oceanic dispersal of hatchlings could explain why the species is restricted to the continental shelf of the northern half of Australia.

Biologists Dr. Scott Eckert and Laura Sarti attach a satellite transmitter to a leatherback turtle on a Pacific beach in Mexico. Satellite tracking is only one of many approaches used by scientists to gather data that can be used to make important decisions regarding the conservation of sea turtles. (Photo © Doug Perrine/Innerspace Visions—Miami)

Conservation—An International Responsibility

Successful sea turtle conservation requires a multifaceted, global approach that includes unilateral and international legislation and agreements, research, and the work of dedicated organizations and individuals. It also means focusing on developing long-term solutions to problems facing sea turtles and reducing reliance on manipulative management methods such as moving nests or raising hatchlings in captivity. Feeding and nesting grounds must be protected, and a public wildlife conservation ethic must be fostered that can withstand vagaries in government regulations, pressure from private interests, and changes in political situations.

Legislation and Agreements

Sea turtles receive protection in the United States under the Endangered Species Act (ESA), which lists the hawksbill, leatherback, and Kemp's ridley as endangered; the green turtle as endangered in Florida and Pacific Mexico and threatened throughout the rest of its range; and the loggerhead as threatened. Inclusion on the list makes it illegal to import, sell, or transport turtles or their products for interstate or foreign commerce. In the United States, the National Marine Fisheries Service has jurisdiction over sea turtles in the water, while the U.S. Fish and Wildlife Service is responsible for them on land. Other countries have their own conservation laws and regulations that apply to sea turtles.

Some regulations affecting sea turtles are global in scope. The Convention on International Trade in Endangered Species of Wild Fauna and Flora (CITES) regulates international trade in endangered and threatened species. Sea turtles are covered under Appendix I of this agreement and ostensibly receive protection from international import and export by all countries that have signed the treaty, although compliance and enforcement leave something to be desired. The Convention on the Conservation of Migratory Species of Wild Animals focuses on endangered species that travel between countries. This convention provides a framework on which to base future conservation agreements, as well as a mechanism for governments to unilaterally conserve endangered migratory species.

Research

Research aimed at understanding the biology, behavior, population trends, and dispersal of sea turtles is needed so that informed management decisions can be made. Tagging studies, satellite tracking of sea turtles, and genetic research are only a few of the scientific approaches used to study sea turtles.

One example illustrating how research can impact wildlife management strategies involves a recent study that used genetic markers to link juvenile loggerheads from nesting beaches in Australia and Japan to their feeding grounds off the coast of Baja California. Several thousand of these loggerheads are killed each year by long-line fisheries in the North Pacific. Nations responsible for the nesting and developmental habitats of marine turtles have jurisdiction over the turtles during migration and on their feeding grounds. The 1983 United Nations Convention on the Conservation of Migratory Species (the Bonn Convention) prohibits the killing of endangered species during migration on the high seas. Though international law bans the killing of sea turtles during migration, the provision is not easily enforced. The results of the study are important because they provide evidence that could be used by Australia, Japan, and Mexico (in association with the appropriate international agencies) to impose limits on the number of turtles that can be killed by the North Pacific long-line fleets.

Participation by Local Populations

Local people must be allowed to participate in and benefit from the protection and management of sea turtles that nest on their shores. Archie Carr recognized this in the 1940s when he established a field station at Tortuguero, Costa Rica, to study green turtles. At that time, villagers slaughtered nearly every turtle that came ashore, taking some of the meat as food for themselves and exporting the calipee. Now the area is part of Tortuguero National Park and draws more than forty-seven thousand visitors each year. With financial backing from the Caribbean Conservation Corporation, the Tortuguero station focuses not only on research and coastal preservation, but also designs programs to help local people benefit from ecotourism without jeopardizing the area's natural values.

Another program in Costa Rica involves the limited legal harvest of olive ridley eggs at Ostional. Ostional is one of the few places in the world where nesting concentrations are so dense that nesting turtles may accidentally dig up the eggs of turtles that nested early in an arribada. Village members of the Asociación Desarrollo Integral de Ostional (ADIO) gather eggs during the first thirty-six hours of each arribada, after which time they protect nests from poachers and the hatchlings from predators. Following approval from the

A Nahuatl Indian boy proudly shows a black turtle hatchling and a leatherback hatchling from a hatchery at Michoacan, Mexico. Villagers dig up turtle nests and move the clutches to hatcheries to protect them from poachers and predators. (Photo © George H. H. Huey)

Ministry of Agriculture and Livestock, biologists at the University of Costa Rica field station determine when the harvest can begin and establish quotas for each arribada. Sometimes conditions dictate that no eggs can be taken; other times, the harvest may approach 35 percent of the eggs that are laid. The premise of the association's controlled harvest is that they collect eggs that would be broken or would stand little chance of

Biologist Kim Cliffton examines a dead leatherback turtle washed up on the sand at Michoacan, Mexico. (Photo © George H. H. Huey)

hatching, thereby increasing the overall productivity of the rookery. Money from the legal sale of the eggs is then pumped back into the community. Although the Ostional project is successful for the community (the program raises more than $95,000 annually), many conservationists are not convinced the take is harmless. Researchers agree Ostional is a unique situation and not one that can likely be used with other species.

A research and conservation project that does have the potential as a model for practical, widespread use focuses on black turtles at Michoacán, Mexico. Here, in the fishing villages of Colola and Maruata, an iguana farm provides meat and cash income once derived from sea turtles. Biologists from the research station teach courses at the local school and hire villagers to protect nests.

An artisans' cooperative teaches crafts and sells pottery to tourists. The villagers realize that without such programs, their turtles would be gone.

The Role of Conservation Organizations

Conservation organizations have been crucial in bridging the gap between research and public education about sea turtles. Their work continues today, and they need the support of people of all ages who believe the welfare of sea turtles and the health of the planet and all its citizens are matters of critical concern.

The Caribbean Conservation Corporation

The Caribbean Conservation Corporation (CCC), a nonprofit organization based in Gainesville, Florida, was the first marine turtle conservation organization in the world and has more than thirty years experience in international sea turtle conservation, research, and education. It was instrumental in promoting the designa-

Confiscated black turtle meat on shore at Michoacan, Mexico. Sea turtles are protected under national and international laws, but enforcement of these laws is difficult. (Photo © George H. H. Huey)

tion of the Tortuguero nesting beach as part of one of Costa Rica's first national parks. Today, the CCC operates the research station and Environmental Education and Interpretation Center at Tortuguero; oversees Tortuguero's Green Turtle Tagging Program; coordinates the International Cooperative Tagging Project with the Archie Carr Center for Sea Turtle Research at the University of Florida; is helping to develop a management plan for the five-thousand-square mile Miskito Coast Protected Area in Nicaragua, which includes one of the largest resident green turtle feeding grounds in the world; and is active in community development programs in Nicaragua designed to benefit the indigenous Miskito people. Such efforts help the Miskito people conserve important habitat to the benefit of sea turtles and the entire ecosystem. In addition, the Sea Turtle Survival League, the CCC's public awareness and environmental education program, has implemented a turtle adoption project to support satellite tracking studies with green turtles; is campaigning to create a special Florida license plate that will raise funds for Florida's Marine Turtle Protection Program and increase awareness about Florida's sea turtles; and is working to help obtain funding to buy land for the Archie Carr National Wildlife Refuge located in east-central Florida.

Ken Goddard of the U.S. Fish and Wildlife Service Forensics Laboratory in Ashland, Oregon, displays a stuffed sea turtle in a room filled with shelves of confiscated sea turtle products. It is illegal in the United States and many other countries to import or export sea turtle products. (Photo © Jeffrey Rich)

The Center for Marine Conservation

Based in Washington, D.C., the Center for Marine Conservation (CMC)—formerly the Center for Environmental Education (CEE)—is the world's leading nonprofit organization devoted solely to the protection of marine wildlife, their habitats, and the conservation of coastal and ocean resources. The CMC promotes sea turtle projects worldwide and played an instrumental role in the banning of international trade in sea turtle products, mandating the use of Turtle Excluder Devices (TEDs) by shrimp trawlers in the United States and other countries, reducing marine debris, and pushing for ordinances regulating beach lighting during turtle nesting seasons.

These are only two organizations out of the hundreds devoted to local, national, and international conservation efforts. Some are very narrow in their focus, such as those concerned only with sea turtle protection, while others have a much broader approach. Yet all are working together in their own way to preserve the intricate and diverse biological fabric that binds all creatures and all ecosystems together.

Habitat protection

Feeding grounds and nesting habitats can be protected through legislation, conservation easements, mitigation, and other such methods. Sometimes the only way to protect habitat, however, is to buy it. This is the case with the Archie Carr National Wildlife Refuge, a sanctuary of undeveloped land in four segments along more than twenty miles of beach between Melbourne and Wabasso on Florida's east coast. This stretch of coastline attracts more nesting loggerheads and green turtles than anywhere else in the United States. Named for Archie Carr because of his tremendous contributions to the understanding and conservation of sea turtles, it is the single most important nesting beach for loggerheads in the Western Hemisphere. It is also the only sea turtle refuge in the United States.

Despite its National Wildlife Refuge designation and ongoing efforts to raise the money to buy the needed land, development threatens the Archie Carr Refuge. By the middle of 1994, only about 30 percent of the proposed 860 acres had been purchased, leaving 70 percent vulnerable to development. The U.S. Fish and Wildlife Service, the state of Florida, Indian River and Brevard Counties, the Sea Turtle Survival League, The Nature Conservancy, the Center for Marine Conservation, and other private groups are working together to purchase the needed land and develop management plans for the area, before it is too late.

Conservation Goals

The problems facing sea turtles are numerous and, for the most part, we are responsible for them. The actions required to address these problems can be outlined as definable goals:

• Crack down on illegal international commerce in sea turtles and their products by enforcing laws and agreements.

• Decrease the loss of turtles to commercial fishing through enforcement of Turtle Excluder Device (TED) and gill net regulations and addressing the problems of drift nets, long lines, and other fishing methods that kill turtles.

- Preserve and restore developmental, feeding, and nesting habitats.
- Make nesting beaches acceptable to turtles by eliminating the impact of artificial lighting, halting shore armoring, and controlling predators.
- Enforce international agreements (such as MARPOL, Annex V) to minimize the dumping of pollutants and solid waste into the ocean.
- Ensure that channel and port dredging, beach and dune restoration projects, and other coastal construction activities are carried out in a manner that does not endanger sea turtles and other wildlife.
- Continue sea turtle research and monitoring activities.
- Increase public awareness and participation in sea turtle conservation through education.

Survivors in a Sea of Change

Sea turtles have witnessed a multitude of environmental events in their lengthy tenure on this planet, including dramatic changes in climate, large fluctuations in sea level, the constantly changing faces of land masses, and the evolution and extinction of millions of other·life forms. Yet it has been only within the last few hundred years that sea turtles have been threatened with complete annihilation at the hands of humans.

Their plight is a reflection of our consumptive attitude toward the environment. The world is *not* our oyster. Our failure to protect sea turtles moves us one step closer to our own encounter with eternity. In the words of a Maruata, Mexico, fisherman as reported in a recent *National Geographic* article, "We don't want to have to tell our children someday that the turtles were here once, but they were all killed." Sea turtles still have so much to teach us. If we open our minds and listen to them with conscience, perhaps they will share with us their most important lesson—the lesson of survival.

Sun rays beam down through the water column as a hawksbill turtle rises toward the surface. (Photo © Doug Perrine/ Innerspace Visions—Miami)

Volunteers collect eggs from a nesting loggerhead turtle to transfer to a hatchery at Cape Florida State Park, Key Biscayne, Florida. (Photo © Doug Perrine/ Innerspace Visions–Miami)

Florida state park rangers, volunteers, and visitors at Cape Florida State Park observe a loggerhead nesting while on a "turtle walk," an event intended to allow participants an opportunity to learn about sea turtles and watch them nest with minimal disturbance to the turtles. (Photo © Doug Perrine/Innerspace Visions–Miami)

Watching Sea Turtles

Guided turtle walks are an increasingly popular mode of educational entertainment. These programs are typically sponsored by conservation organizations such as The Nature Conservancy, or by state or federal agencies such as the National Park Service or Florida Department of Environmental Protection. The programs usually take place in the evening and begin with an educational slide show identifying the various species of sea turtles, explaining aspects of their life history, and discussing the problems that face them. A guide then takes you out on the beach to observe a sea turtle as she lays her eggs. Guided programs are the best way to see nesting turtles, eggs, and sometimes hatchlings up close. Some groups offer volunteer opportunities, such as at The Nature Conservancy's Blowing Rocks Preserve on Jupiter Island, Florida, or at the Caribbean Conservation Corporation's Tortuguero research facility in Costa Rica.

Whether you see a nesting sea turtle on your own during an evening stroll on the beach or while observing with a guided group, there are precautions you should take to ensure that your visit does not inadvertently cause the turtle to abandon her nest or deter other turtles from coming ashore. Don't use a flashlight on the beach or take flash photographs. Walk as close to the water's edge as possible so that you don't surprise a turtle as she is crawling up the beach or beginning to dig. If you see a turtle in the surf, crouch down low, and don't approach her. Otherwise, she may turn around and head back to sea. If you see a turtle up on the beach, stay at least one hundred feet (30 m) away and to the rear of the turtle; never approach her head or get in front of her. Never disturb or harass a nesting turtle by making noise, shining lights, or trying to ride her. Watch where you step if you are walking the beach when hatchlings are emerging; they seem to come from nowhere and you don't want to crush one accidentally.

Even if you never see a turtle on a nesting beach, there are things you can do to help them. Never buy products made from sea turtles or other endangered species. It is illegal to bring them into the United States (and into many other countries), and it creates a demand for these products, which encourages poaching. Keep informed about current marine turtle issues, and support legislation that protects sea turtles. Write or phone elected officials to encourage them to support sea turtle conservation. You can also support or volunteer with conservation organizations that are active in sea turtle issues and habitat protection, such as The Nature Conservancy, the Center for Marine Conservation, or the Sea Turtle Survival League of the Caribbean Conservation Corporation. Sea turtle conservation is a responsibility we all must share and a cause in which we all can participate.

Index

References

Baker, Christopher P. "Hatching Their Eggs and Eating Them, Too." *Pacific Discovery* (47)3:10–18, Summer 1994.

Bjorndal, Karen A. (editor), *Biology and Conservation of Sea Turtles*. Washington, D.C.: Smithsonian Institution Press in cooperation with World Wildlife Fund, Inc., 1981.

————. "Nutritional Ecology of Sea Turtles." *Copeia* 1985(3): 736–751.

Bowen, Brian W. et al. "Global Population Structure and Natural History of the Green Turtle (*Chelonia mydas*) in Terms of Matriarchal Phylogeny." *Evolution* 46(4), 865–881, 1992.

————. et al. "Trans-Pacific Migrations of the Loggerhead Turtle (*Caretta caretta*) Demonstrated with Mitochondrial DNA Markers." Unpublished document.

Caribbean Conservation Corporation. *Velador: The Caribbean Conservation Corporation Newsletter.*

Carr, Archie. *The Sea Turtle: So Excellent a Fishe*. Austin: The University of Texas Press, 1967, 1984.

————. *The Windward Road: Adventures of a Naturalist on Remote Caribbean Shores*. Tallahassee: The Florida State University Press, 1955, 1979.

Cornelius, Stephen E., *The Sea Turtles of Santa Rosa National Park*. Costa Rica: Fundacion de Parques Nacionales, 1986.

Grossman, Dan and Seth Shulman. "Earthly Attractions." *Earth* 4(1): 34–41, February 1995.

Lahiri, S. et al. "Application of a Mixed Stock Analysis to the Demography of Atlantic and Mediterranean Loggerhead Turtles." Unpublished document.

Limpus, Colin J. et al. "The Flatback Turtle, *Chelonia depressa*, in Queensland: Post Nesting Migration and Feeding Ground Distribution." *Australian Wildlife Research* 1983(10): 557–561.

Lutz, Peter L. and Timothy B. Bentley. "Respiratory Physiology of Diving in the Sea Turtle." *Copeia* 1985(3): 671–679.

Meylan, Anne Barkau. "Riddle of the Ridleys." *Natural History,* 90–96, November 1986.

National Research Council, *Decline of the Sea Turtles: Causes and Prevention*. Washington, D.C.: National Academy Press, 1990.

Pritchard, P. C. H. *Encyclopedia of Turtles*. Neptune, N.J.: T. F. H. Publications, 1979.

Richardson, T. H., J. I. Richardson, and M. Donnelly (Compilers). *Proceedings of the Tenth Annual Workshop on Sea Turtle Biology and Conservation*. NOAA Technical Memorandum NMFS-SEFC-278. 1990.

Rudloe, Jack. *Time of the Turtle*. New York: Alfred A. Knopf, 1979.

Rudloe, Jack and Anne. "Sea Turtles: In a Race for Survival." *National Geographic* 185(2): 94–121, February 1994.

Salmon, M. and J. Wynekan (Compilers). *Proceedings of the Eleventh Annual Workshop on Sea Turtle Biology and Conservation*. NOAA Technical Memorandum NMFS-SEFSC-302. 1991.

Schroeder, B. A. and B. E. Witherington (Compilers). *Proceedings of the Thirteenth Annual Symposium on Sea Turtle Biology and Conservation*. NOAA Technical Memorandum NMFS-SEFSC-341. 1994.

Spotila, James R. and Edward A. Standora. "Environmental Constraints on the Thermal Energetics of Sea Turtles." *Copeia* 1985(3): 694–702.

————. "Temperature Dependent Sex Determination in Sea Turtles." *Copeia* 1985(3): 711–722.

Van Meter, Victoria B. *Florida's Sea Turtles*. Florida Power and Light Company, 1992.

Walker, T. A. "Juvenile Flatback Turtles in Proximity to Coastal Nesting Islands in the Great Barrier Reef Province." *Journal of Herpetology* 25(2): 246–248, 1991.

Walker, T. A. and C. J. Parmenter. "Absence of a Pelagic Phase in the Life Cycle of the Flatback Turtle, *Natator depressa* (Garman)." *Journal of Biogeography* 17: 275–278, 1990.

Zangerl, Rainer, L. P. Hendrickson, and J. R. Hendrickson. *A Redescription of the Australian Flatback Sea Turtle*. Honolulu: Bishop Museum Press, 1988.

About the Author

(Photo © John Adkins)

Jeff Ripple, natural history writer and photographer, spends much of his time exploring the wilds of his home state, Florida, with notebook and camera in hand. He is the author of *Big Cypress Swamp and the Ten Thousand Islands* (University of South Carolina Press, 1992) and *The Florida Keys: The Natural Wonders of an Island Paradise* (Voyageur Press, 1995). Jeff lives with his wife, Renée, and their cats Tabatha and Suwannee on eight wooded acres near Gainesville, Florida.